Simple, Not Easy

Simple, Not Easy

Reflections on community, social responsibility and tolerance

Terrence Roberts

of the Little Rock Nine

Parkhurst Brothers, Inc., Publishers

MARION, MICHIGAN

PARKHURST BROTHERS, INC., PUBLISHERS

Our National Conversation
Raising the level of public discourse

www.parkhurstbrothers.com

Parkhurst Brothers books are distributed to the trade through the Chicago Distribution Center, a unit of the University of Chicago Press, and may be ordered through Ingram Book Company, Baker & Taylor, Follett Library Resources and other book industry wholesalers. To order from the University of Chicago's Chicago Distribution Center, phone 1-800-621-847 or send a fax to 800-621-2736. Copies of this and other Parkhurst Brothers Inc., Publishers titles are available to organizations and corporations for purchase in quantity by contacting Special Sales Department at our home office location, listed on our web site.

Printed in the United States of America. First Paperback Edition, 2022

12 11 10 9 8 7 6 5 4 3 2 1

Library of Congress Control Number: 2009942594

ISBN: Paperback 978-1-62491-163-7
ISBN: Hardcover 978-1-935166-16-0
ISBN: e-book 978-1-935166-26-9

This book is printed on archival-quality paper that meets requirements of the American National Standard for Information Sciences, Permanence of Paper, Printed Library Materials, ANSI Z39.48-1984.

Design Director and Dustjacket/cover design:
WENDELL E. HALL

Page design:

SHELLY CULBERTSON

Acquired for Parkhurst Brothers Inc., Publishers by:
TED PARKHURST

Editor:
ROGER ARMBRUST

Proofreaders:
BILL AND BARBARA PADDACK

DEDICATION

I dedicate this book to my wife, Rita (known to me, most family members and some friends as Jeanie), a constant and consistent muse for me throughout our married life. Words are truly inadequate to communicate how much better a person I am because of her. She knows me, and still loves me! What a gift!

ACKNOWLEDGMENTS

Any project of this nature is produced by a virtual army of people.

My heartfelt thanks to all who have invited me to share with their student bodies, commencement audiences, Martin Luther King, Jr., Day celebrants, congregations, and professional conference attendees. You made it possible for me to connect with succeeding generations through telling my story, sharing insights, and bearing witness to the need for more passionate involvement in life's journey. Countless others have contributed in tangible and intangible ways, and their influence will be seen and felt throughout this book. To all I owe a tremendous debt of gratitude.

I would like to also thank my publisher, Ted Parkhurst, whose vision and inspiration has opened a whole new world for me to explore. It was his idea that we use *Simple, Not Easy* as a title. Roger Armbrust's editing skills have made this work much more substantive. His keen eye for detail and ability to pare excess verbiage is without parallel. Publicist Lauren Roddy has labored to make this work known in wider and wider circles. Prolific author Paul Robert Walker has been instrumental in helping me understand more about the publishing process; he connected me and Ted.

Table of Contents

9 Preface

15 In Quest of Truth: Exploding the Mythology of Our Times

23 Always Tell the Truth (But, don't always be telling it!)

29 Navigating Life's Terrain

37 Choosing to Lead an Ethical Life

45 Lessons from Little Rock

59 Reflections on Life in Little Rock

71 Caring Enough to Confront

79 Choosing Nonviolence: The Courage to be Different

87 Creating the Beloved Community

93 Reshaping the Mental Map: Cross-Cultural Life in the 21st Century

99 Relationships Across Lines of Demarcation

103 Self: The Most Important Tool in Multicultural Intervention

113 Life in the 21st Century: Coping with a Legacy of Racism

121 Education: A Power Tool for the 21st Century

125 Seeking to Explain Clarence

131 Regarding Daisy: Thoughts Drafted in Anticipation of a Celebration of Life

133 Philander Smith College Remarks

139 The Ongoing Battle for Equality

143 Remarks Delivered at the U.S. Postal Service

145 Letter to Philander Smith College Athletes

147 Remarks at Facing History Benefit Dinner

151 A Brief Note about Committing to Fifth-Level Living

153 The Value of True Education

159 Building Relationships: A Christian Perspective

163 Can There Be Any Good Thing Here?

167 In Search of an Open Mind

169 On the Inauguration of Neal King as President of Antioch University

173 Letter to Sen. Barack Obama, Democratic Presidential Candidate

175 President Barack Obama: Thoughts and Reflections

183 Endnotes

Preface

These writings represent a portion of the ideas, notions, reflections, and conclusions I have committed to paper over the past 20-plus years. The subject matter ranges widely. It includes thoughts about education, leadership, racial integration in schools and neighborhoods, race and racism. I discuss the importance of building community, and ethical decision-making to commitment, truth-telling, and the battle for equality in the United States, the essence of affirmative action. I also express my thoughts about some folk considered to be influential citizens. You will find a voice consistently trying to find answers to vexing questions, and posing challenges to the current status quo. In my assessment, nothing here might be deemed radical, although you might find my diatribe directed toward Supreme Court Justice Clarence Thomas rather pointed. That aside, these writings aim, primarily, to underscore important issues, and challenge you, the reader, to think beyond the ordinary.

All of human activity takes place within the context of relationship. With this thought in mind, I attempt here to build a relationship with you, the reader. For a relationship to proceed with any degree of success, we must communicate sufficiently well enough to convey meaning to each other. Since this is written material, the conversation will be, initially, one-sided. You may be moved, later, to write to me about one thing or another. Then the dialogue can grow and develop into a full-fledged human encounter. For instance, you may disagree with points I make, or with my tone, or with some other aspect of my thinking; it's at that point I relish your feedback. Or, you may agree with many things I have to say and wish to connect with a kindred spirit—an encounter I welcome as well.

Here's a fantasy of mine: that real change can occur only when we build strong dyads, which then become the foundational blocks for new societies. Our interaction could very well constitute one such block.

You will discover early in this reading that I am partial to certain schemes and constructs. By the time you reach the final pages, you will become well acquainted with the "Four-Step Process." I'll review "The Parable of the Geese Children." I'll highlight my life in Little Rock, as well as my year-long ordeal at Central High School, along with too many "favorite phrases" and "favorite authors" to mention. That said, I promise not to bore you, because I cannot abide tedious printed matter, and will not inflict any such thing on you. (You may well disagree!! And if you do, I apologize in advance, and will strive to make the next volume more appealing.)

I haven't presented the works in chronological order, but instead I've grouped them based on themes and kinds of presentations. Further, I've chosen these entries because they represent the kinds of essays, lectures, and sermons that I have written during years past. The essay written in 1989 represents the earliest in this collection. Its focus is race and racism.

I have given talks about Martin Luther King, Jr., each January or February for as long as I can remember, and I have included three of those talks here: "Caring Enough to Confront," "Choosing Non-Violence: The Courage to be Different," and "Creating the Beloved Community." These will give you a fairly comprehensive look at my thoughts about the impact and influence of Dr. King on our society.

The address I gave at the Huntington Library in San Marino, California, is virtually the same one I gave a year later in Salisbury, Maryland. I've included both because I feel that together they help you, the reader, to understand better the year I spent at Central High School in Little Rock, Arkansas. There are nuances and details that do not appear in both, but they are essential enough for me to present them together. Part of the reason is that, even though I don't like the idea of the "stump speech," this qualifies as one for me. I realize that I can't change the facts, but I can change the way in which the facts are presented, a matter of style for me. And I hope this all makes sense to you.

I've grouped graduation speeches together, as well as sermons and related talks to church groups. There are only two entries in this latter category, although there were lots more to choose from. During the time I spent in Southern Illinois (1972-1975), I was an elder in my local church. The pastor was a circuit preacher with several churches in the area. When he was away, the elders had to provide the morning sermons. I have in mind writing a separate book focused more on spiritual matters, so I will save those writings for that publication.

I am invited often to address groups at various places and speak on topics that relate to their mission or program theme. I've included three entries that represent such talks. The first of the trio, "Reshaping the Mental Map: Cross-Cultural Life in the 21st Century," was presented to the U.S. Department of Veterans Affairs in Sepulveda, California, on January 27, 1993. The organizers were interested in hearing my take on cross-cultural issues and how we might respond to them. Ultimately they wanted to know how to help their constitutients manage life in an increasingly more complex cultural environment.

The San Bernardino, California, Unified School District invited me to address a group of educators about similar issues on August 18, 2000. My topic for that presentation was: "Relationships Across Lines of Demarcation." The participants were keenly interested in how to help students cope with difference. Incidents of black on brown violence were escalating and teachers and administrators were looking for answers.

The third and final talk in this section was delivered at the Biennial Conference of the Multicultural Research and Training Lab of Pepperdine University on Saturday October 11, 2008. The title chosen for this presentation was: "Self: The Most Important Tool in Multicultural Intervention." The audience was composed of graduate students in education and psychology and their professors. My attempt was to reinforce the notion that self is the most salient tool as clinicians seek to intervene in the lives of fellow humans. I started to pay close attention to this factor as a graduate student in social welfare in the early '60s. It made sense then and continues to inform the work I do in clinical settings.

Some pieces here don't fit neatly into categories; the one that comes to mind quickly is "Seeking to Understand Clarence." I was so angry with George the First for placing this man on the U.S. Supreme Court, I had to find an outlet for my frustrations; this essay is the result. Maybe I've included it to stimulate dialogue; I am more than interested in what others think and feel about Justice Thomas. For me, the seat occupied by Thurgood Marshall was sacred. It seemed sacrilegious to offer it to Clarence, who seemed not to embody any of the passion for human justice that I had witnessed in Justice Marshall.

There are several shorter pieces included here, and they appear together just for convenience. Except for the six entries focused on aspects of life in Little Rock, no obvious threads tie them together; each one will speak to you on its own merits.

I thank you for taking the time to read these writings. I trust they will prove useful in your quest for more complete understanding of life's concerns and issues.

I start this collection of narratives with three talks given at college graduation ceremonies, and one talk given to graduating high-school seniors. One of my preferred assignments involves speaking to students. To college graduates, I cite the essentials they need as they prepare to take positions in the economic, political, social, and spiritual milieu of our times; I do likewise with high-school seniors, poised to take the next step in their quest for formal education. Hopefully, if I have done my job well enough, the words I have shared with the graduates will resonate with you, the reader, as well.

"In Quest of Truth: Exploding the Mythology of Our Times," is my address to the graduating class of the School of Education at the University of Redlands on May 29, 2003. Educators, especially, have a distinct role to play in this process of debunking myths. And, I must point out that all of us share this responsibility to develop awareness of and to confront the prevailing mythology around us.

At the Pacific Oaks College graduation on June 4, 2005, I chose to entitle my remarks "Always Tell the Truth (But, Don't Always Be Telling It!)" Sound advice for the general populace, too, given the problems we have with communication! Remember the old adage, "Never cast your pearls before swine?" Maybe that's what I had in mind with this address. I'd like to know what you think about it.

And thirdly, I presented "Navigating Life's Terrain" to the graduating class of Fullerton College on May 22, 2008. My main thrust: encouraging the graduates to begin thinking about the tools needed to meet life's post-college demands. In all three of these presentations, I intended to inspire, uplift, challenge, and motivate the graduating students to take life seriously; to commit to being involved in the fray, and to avoid having to "risk the peril of being judged not to have lived."

The final entry in this section is the talk I gave to the seniors at Westridge Academy in Pasadena, California, on June 9, 2006: "Choosing to Lead an Ethical Life." It seemed appropriate for me to challenge this elite group to think seriously about the need for ethical behavior in today's world: a society prone to cutting corners, and rounding off the edges of integrity in an effort to create acceptable rationales for the self-enhancing schemes that threaten to weaken, if not destroy, our foundational principles.

Young people of today will very soon become our world's leaders. I, for one, want them to take responsibility for the choices they make, and to make those choices by considering the welfare and well-being of us all. This train of thought informed my writing as I prepared each of the four talks you will read next in this volume.

Terrence Roberts
Pasadena, California

In Quest of Truth: Exploding the Mythology of Our Times

Commencement address delivered to
the graduating class of The School of Education,
University of Redlands

May 29, 2003

The role of educators in our society is clearly delineated for me. At the outset we must recognize our sacred trust. We hold positions of some power and authority; we can influence, persuade, direct, and model behavior for others. We can help them determine exactly how to be in this universe. But perhaps more than any of these things is the charge to dispel myth and uphold the truth as we know it. Not an easy task, especially in the face of what seems to be a general preference for mythological explanations of reality. As one glaring example, we can investigate the mythological construct of race in our society.

The truth of the matter is this: I simply don't remember when it was that I discovered race. You know the old axiom about fish not knowing the nature of water; well, that's about the way it was for me down in the Arkansas delta region, down in Little Rock and its near environs. All of life was about race; it was around me, everywhere; nobody knew anything different. In fact, all of life was connected in some deep and lasting way with this notion of race. Race dictated who was welcomed into the halls of government, into the laboratories of production, into the classrooms, the entertainment centers, the neighborhoods of affluence, and all positions of power and influence in the community.

This is not to say that all were not truly welcomed somewhere, but there were mandatory conditions imposed according to your racial group membership. And everybody seemed to know who belonged to what group in spite of the fact that the rules of race were not written down anywhere. Oh, there were laws to be sure, laws that said black and white shall forever be separate; but in point of fact, that never happened. Black people and white people played by a set of unwritten rules that spelled out the ways in which they would, indeed, interact. It was all about racial hierarchy, and as long as black people accepted their place at the rear of lines, the backs of busses, the balconies of theaters, etc., there was no problem. The mythology of race was such that whiteness was held to be superior to blackness, and as long as this seemed to be the order of the day, chaos and disruption were held at bay. Fortunately for me, my mom explained the mythology of race while I was still quite young. She told me that race was simply a man-made artifact. This helped immensely to bring clarity to this otherwise very foggy notion.

My mom ran a catering business out of our home, and I was employed often as a cook's helper. We would prepare food and take it to the kitchens of white home owners, serve the guests, and clean the kitchen before we departed for our side of town. We were welcomed into their kitchens and dining rooms as servants, but we could not, based on the mythology of race, be included in their guest lists for dinner. This was puzzling for me, this unreasonable way of dividing up the world, color-coding it, if you will. I had been immersed in the mythology of the way things were "spozed to be." And they remained that way until the Supreme Court decision in 1954, until the law of the land changed dramatically, and the color line was singled out for erasure.

Now here was something I could get my hands around. Here was a new thing worthy of being investigated and analyzed for the possibilities it suggested, for the potential for radical change it portended. I was ecstatic in the wake of the Brown decision. This 1954 decision in Brown v. Board of Education did not expressly overrule Plessy v. Ferguson, the old "separate but equal" decision rendered by the Supreme Court in 1896; but the Court did conclude that "in the field of public education the doctrine of separate but equal has no place." But it was the Brown decision that had a direct impact on my life and the way in which I began to view the operations in the legal arena, especially with respect to civil rights. My own study led me to analyze the findings in a number of cases. The citation Roberts v. City of Boston got my attention because of the likelihood that an ancestor of mine might have been the plaintiff. In this 1849 Massachusetts case, the Massachusetts Supreme Court upheld the right of the Boston School Committee to make separate provision for the "instruction of colored children." What stands out here for me, in addition to the Court's use of race as a limiting factor, is the need for black people to use extraordinary energy and time to bring these issues to the public discourse.

The Plessy decision made it crystal clear to all that this country was not yet ready to grant equality to black people. I was heartened by the Brown decision, but disappointed with the "all deliberate speed" caveat imposed by the Court. And yet, in spite of this mixed message, the Little Rock School Board deemed it appropriate to move forward in compliance with Brown. As their plan was revealed, my hand was raised high in eager anticipation; I was ready for change. You see, the mythology of race held that white kids were smarter than black kids, that black people were subhuman and could not learn. I knew otherwise, of course, but my presence at Central High School would serve to alert others to the mythological character of race. We did not enter Central with a primary goal of dispelling the myth, but it would happen simply as a consequence of our presence. As we challenged the myth, as we demonstrated the foolishness of the construct, it would vanish into thin air. Sadly, it did not work out as planned. Race still commands a legion of followers. Our task in this new century is to put the myth to rest forever, to communicate to the misinformed and the ill-advised the efficacy of erasing the mythology of race from their mental maps.

In truth, this issue of race is part and parcel of our inability to cope with difference of any sort. The very idea of difference seems to trigger responses and reactions that indicate a certain caution about whatever or whoever it is that wears the "different" label. This is occasioned primarily by the fact that we are all unique beings in this universe, and whatever or whoever is not *us* tends to fall under intense scrutiny. Add to this scenario the tendency to use subjective criteria in our analysis of the other, and you wind up with the reality we face today: a society defined by lines of separation based on perceived differentness.

There are, of course, complexities and exceptions, and unusual circumstances; but, in the main, we live in spaces outlined by the lines of demarcation. How much longer will it take for us to figure out that the one thing we have in common is difference? Often I am confronted by those who would have us voluntarily disable ourselves and become color-blind, as they put it. I fail to see the efficacy of such a choice, since the beauty of difference would be obliterated. Difference simply is. There is nothing one need do to make difference palatable; at least that's my bias. Personally, I enjoy difference, and look forward to each new encounter. The mythology of sameness reigns supreme, however, in spite of all the evidence to the contrary. Not that I attempt to convert the masses to my point of view, but the fact remains, my DNA is not your DNA! That's why I say we have difference in common; we can be tracked through the universe by the DNA spoor left on our trail as we meander through life. Yes, sameness is indeed a myth, and we need not despair about that reality. In fact, for me at least, there is a sense of great satisfaction and contentment, because I know that the universe is not complete on any given day until I have made my own unique contribution. And I look forward to the contributions of others as well.

In much the same way, we have seen thus far the mythological notion of equality of opportunity takes up space in the collective mental maps of vast numbers of red-blooded Americans. It seems to be an article of faith for some who speak assertively about the certainty of this as a true and unwavering concept. For those true believers, there is no need to question whether the thing is here or not; for them it exists a priori, part of the great I AM! Any evidence to the contrary is explained away as being proof positive that individuals simply do not take advantage of the ubiquitous opportunities that lie in wait. To bolster arguments for this myth, and to counter arguments against it, this rabid, yellow-dog, folklore spouting, flag-waving, dyed-in-the-wool believer offers countless anecdotal tales. With them he aims to prove to the (most likely left-leaning) skeptic that anybody who wants to, by God!, can do whatever, whenever, and however in this hallowed ground we so reverently call America.

It is often, in just such arenas of near uncontrolled bluster, that I come, dripping sweet reason, and pose this simple paradox: Why then, in this land of opportunity for all, have we not ever elected a female to the office of President of these United States? You see, it seems to me that if there were such a thing as equality of opportunity, there should have been, at some point in all of our years of historical existence, a woman at the helm. Well, for one thing, it makes statistical sense. All of us can count, and when we add up the numbers, it looks awfully suspicious to find that we have managed to avoid electing a woman to occupy the White House. How does such a thing come to be? I say it is because the myth is not the reality; the reality is that we do not have equality of opportunity. And no matter how high up you place the myth, it is still a myth. A much more objective view is that some of us have opportunities, and some of us do not. But, even more insidious, we *know* who will have the opportunities and who will not! Oh yes, there are exceptions. There have always been exceptions to the rule; but in the main, the myth spells out with brutal clarity who gets tapped for the perks, the positions, the promotions, the possibilities. And, that gratuitous alliteration aside, it is hard to dislodge the mythological thinking.

Another myth very closely related to this one is the idea that we have in place a meritocracy, a system of rewards based on meritorious achievement. Some would have us believe that high-school seniors line up across America according to their SAT scores, and that college admissions officers start at the top and work downward to fill the first-year openings. Not true.

First, we must consider that little matter of outstanding athletic ability. A poor SAT score can be offset if the applicant for one of the ever-diminishing college entry slots can show evidence of having a consistently accurate jump shot, or has been known to run the 100-yard dash in ten seconds or less. In fact, it is this group of physically endowed high schoolers, having excelled in a variety of sporting activities, who get the nod from admissions officers before others are even considered.

And immediately following this first cut, the search is on for those applicants whose parents and/or grandparents have contributed large sums of money to the college or university. The third tier is reserved for those applicants who are the progeny of alumni.

Higher education is big business in the minds of many. Of course, this flies in the face of all the platitudinous rhetoric in support of the notion of meritocracy. Work hard, pull yourself up by your bootstraps, burn the midnight oil—all these sentiments are designed to convince young people that they have a chance to reach the highest pinnacles of success in our society.

The mythological character of the construct is evident when we look closely at the core, when we probe the essence of the thing. It is not about merit, but about a whole complex of things often beyond the reach of the ordinary citizen. We must consider the benefits conferred upon those who have immediate access to the leaders in business and industry, to those who have personal ties to politicians, who count among their intimates those who influence policy decisions in all spheres of our social, legal, economic, and justice systems. The deal made on the golf course, the casual recommendation for a summer internship made over lunch, the phone call to Judge So-and-so on behalf of "that fine young man who was here for dinner last night." These are not there for the meritorious taking by all who would aspire to greatness.

The reality is that we have a system of favoritism, not one of merit. And yet, the myth has secured a rather permanent place in our society, in our psyche. It is believed by legions, and preached by many others with fervor and dedication. Perhaps the goal is to speak the words so loudly that they become, over time, real and unassailable. But no matter the impetus, simply know this: We have not yet attained the Nirvana of meritocracy.

I acknowledge, readily, that one man's mythology is another man's seminal truth. But is it not so that we have not yet asked the necessary questions about our cherished beliefs? And surely, one such question would be, is this myth or reality? I submit that even as we know without doubt that polar bears are black[1], we continue to identify them as white because of the prevalence of the myth. It is time to confront the mythology of our world, to bring light and truth to the fore, and to set this society on a course leading to the realization of its potential to be great, rather than one leading us to certain ruin and destruction.

The hard work of learning how to do this includes making changes in the structure of our mental maps, those devices we use to make sense out of the universe. In the arena of difference, we will find it necessary to redefine, reconstruct, rethink, and reevaluate our approach to those deemed different from self. As we experience the gradual fading of the lines that separate us, as we diligently erase those markers, we will discover the magic of living without confining boundaries. Collectively we can transcend the status quo, and demonstrate to the world that it's possible to overcome mythology, and replace it with a truth too compelling to ignore. Inevitably there will be resistance to what some may count as a demand to pledge allegiance to philosophies and principles that fall too far outside the comfort zone.

But, if what we are proposing is healthy for the body, if difference deserves a place of honor, if truth is preferred over myth, if we are committed to equality for all, then I say let's learn how to make the necessary changes. And then let us go forth from this place with renewed vigor, and preach a gospel that has the power to truly transform our own lives, and ultimately the lives of all those who enter our life space.

Always Tell the Truth (But, don't always be telling it!)

Talk presented to the graduating class of Pacific Oaks College

Saturday, June 4, 2005

Recently I listened to Walter Moseley as he addressed the assembled crowd at California Technical University in Pasadena, California, during one of the University's lecture-series presentations. Mr. Moseley, a novelist of some note and a man with a keen eye for the kind of detail that makes for good reading, suggested that we try to tell the truth, at least once per day. He acknowledged how hard a task this would be for most of us, but encouraged us to do it anyway. As he spoke his words, I was reminded of an early mentor who said to me at one time, "Terry, always tell the truth, but don't always be telling it." These two assignments seem related somehow. At the heart of each is the need to speak the truth. The latter adds a caution that truth telling might best be done only at propitious times, at times when windows of understanding and appreciation are open and minds are receptive. Both allude also to difficulties associated with this seemingly universally acceptable mode of behavior. I mean, who wouldn't want to know and to tell the truth? Why is it so hard a thing to do? The more I thought about this, the more I became convinced that we needed to spend time today investigating the art and science of truth telling.

Some things popped into mind immediately: things like "political correctness," "stretching the truth," "putting on the best face," "avoiding socially embarrassing moments." But none of these things seemed to have anything to do with telling the truth; they all seemed to be strategies for avoiding truth telling. The obvious question was why this cluster of thoughts and not some other? A few seconds of reflection gave me the answer: We are trained, generally, not in the art of reporting the facts as they are, but in the artifice of bending the facts to fit a desired reality.

As an example, our national narrative is one that describes a utopian ideal, a goal for us to lean toward perhaps, but not yet realized. Too often, however, this grand rhetoric fills the air waves, the media pages, and the billboards, constitutes the sound bites, flows freely from academic podiums, religious pulpits and political stumps, and seeks to convince us that Nirvana has indeed arrived. This manufactured text is presented as fact: Anybody can grow up to be President of these United States; all people are created equal; in this system of meritocracy hard work and education will result in the bestowal of appropriate rewards; you could pull yourself up by your bootstraps, if you really wanted to, etc., etc., etc. Noisy, ubiquitous, intrusive, and extremely seductive, this train of thought is often accompanied by built in resistance to any other way of thinking or believing.

Having been baptized by immersion in these same waters, I too was a firm believer in the national narrative. Upon hearing the gospel of manifest destiny as a fourth grader, I was a ready convert. America for Americans, Christianize the heathen, root out the filthy commies, two cars in every garage, one wage-earning dad, one stay-at-home mom, two kids, one dog, and a picket fence, a white picket fence. It was a package deal, and I was told it was the best thing going.

Fortunately I learned to read, and at some point I learned to think; and then the whole fabric began to unravel. At first I thought that the narrative was simply incomplete, that sins of omission had occurred, and it was just a matter of filling in the blank spots. My naiveté knew no bounds. I was a slow learner by some standards, but once I understood how much more there was to be discovered, my need to know was insatiable.

And what a journey it has been! I now see with different eyes, hear with different ears, sense things that before would have been outside my sensory range. In his memoir *South To a Very Old Place*, Albert Murray writes about having a set of antennae that enables him to take readings of his surround, and to determine if truth is being spoken in his presence. That resonates with me. On this trail of discovery I have found that far too many people would rather not challenge the status quo. They think, and feel, that while the national narrative may be less than substantive, it is better than what might be found in other countries or other nations. This rather specious comparative analysis was at first confusing to me. But now I see it simply as a tactic of obfuscation—an attempt to redirect the dialogue, to protect the sanctity of a chosen way of life.

It was this mode of thought that led to the circumstance of United States Representative Barbara Lee being left out on a long, tenuous limb in the wake of her questions about the proposed invasion of Iraq. It was in fear of the consequences of speaking his truth openly that led W. Mark Felt to assume the mysterious persona of Deep Throat. President Kennedy's minions hid in the eye of Hurricane Groupthink while "we the people" approached the brink of nuclear disaster in the Bay of Pigs. What might have been the results in each of these cases if truth had been told, openly and completely? My great fear is that we will never reach such a plateau.

But yet, I am hopeful beyond measure as I look into the faces of the graduating class of 2005. I know from my association with Pacific Oaks College that your courses of study have prompted each one of you to ask the hard questions: to challenge policies, practices, and protocols that threaten to keep us corralled like so many sheep inside fences built by those who fear voices of dissent. It is clear also that you understand the need to seek the truth by any means necessary; that you are not afraid to go naked to the mirror, to face yourself and see what changes and alterations in your mental maps must be accomplished before you venture forth to take your place in the body politic. And as you do so, you will pepper your conversations with Darfur, Jakarta, Thailand, Malawi, Peshawar, Pakistan, Zimbabwe, Rwanda, or other regions of the global community where people are starving and dying in what can only be described as incredible isolation from those of us who have enough to eat, a place to sleep, clean water to drink, and sanitation systems that keep us safely removed from the stench and bacterial ooze of open waste pits.

Your efforts will be directed also toward building community, seeking to include all others. Any line of demarcation between people will be seen as blight on the landscape; and you will bring out your giant Pacific Oaks College eraser, and begin to eradicate yet another barrier keeping people at arm's length from one another.

In writing about community, M. Scott Peck rightly points out that the journey from pseudo-community, where most of us live, to a state of true community will require that we endure the inevitable chaos that such a disruptive choice insures. But your commitment will allow you to create whatever mechanisms are required to master this task.

You have studied the words of Dr. Martin Luther King, Jr., who wrote in his "Letter from Birmingham Jail": "Moreover I am cognizant of the interrelatedness of all communities and states. I cannot sit idly by in Atlanta and not be concerned about what happens in Birmingham. Injustice anywhere is a threat to justice everywhere. We are caught in an inescapable network of mutuality, tied in a single garment of destiny. Whatever affects one directly, affects all indirectly." This excerpt from King's response to critics who saw him as an unwelcome outsider in Birmingham supports our expanded perception of the notion of community.

And how do we experience this notion of true community? Well, for one thing, we *affirm* each member. Through vehicles of positive relationships, we support individual endeavor; we offer incentives for goal-oriented behavior. It was this kind of thinking that led the Founding Fathers to introduce a program of affirmative action for white males. They saw the efficacy of creating a program to insure that all members of that category were given the tools of success. And it worked! The affirmative-action program for white males is the most comprehensive, the most effective, and the most enduring program of affirmative action ever devised by human beings.

You are called upon to bear witness, to give testimony that opens doors of understanding. As you find your way, as you figure out how to navigate this uncertain terrain, you will—by virtue of your very presence and existence—speak some kind of truth. Your actions and words will be seen and heard; and this totality of your communication to others will be perceived not always as you intended. But, that aside, keep leaning in the direction of honest expression.

Resist the temptation to give in for the sake of personal gain or public acclaim. Be willing to work unstintingly in the name of nudging this country toward fulfillment of its promise of full, meaningful life, unfettered liberty, and justice for each and every one of its inhabitants.

This is especially meaningful to me now that my grandson has joined the universe. His personal history now spans just a bit more than two years, and his future is tied inexorably to yours. For his sake, if nothing else, commit your time, energy, soul, and body to the creation of a society that allows all of us to stand with hands over hearts and repeat—not from rote memory and a sense of public duty—but from a bone-marrow conviction that truth is being spoken: "One nation, under God, indivisible, with liberty and justice for all."

Navigating Life's Terrain

Graduation talk presented to Fullerton College
Fullerton, California

Thursday, May 22, 2008

At the time ordained by the hand that guides the universe, you tumble out of the womb and step into a drama already underway. Somebody is designated as primary caretaker for you, and through this person comes your beginning knowledge about your role in this production called life. You learn your name and the part you are to play, and if you are lucky, you may land a starring role. On the other hand, you may be relegated to the edges of the action; bit parts and occasional cameo appearances may be your plight.

In my case the drama was confusing and filled with dialogue that was incoherent. One message I received suggested that my costume was all wrong. I had shown up clad in all black, but it was made perfectly clear to me that the garb most preferred was white. Immediately I faced a dilemma that seemed to have no readily discernible resolution. News of my birth was reported in the local daily newspaper, the *Arkansas Gazette.* All of the babies born in and around Little Rock were presented to the public in that week of December 3, 1941. The list starts off: "Mr. and Mrs. Marcus Spotswood Billingsley, 1309 Main Street, daughter, Geraldine Juliette, Dec. 16." The list continues, non-alphabetically, until an abrupt change occurs about halfway down the page. At this juncture, the obligatory social titles of Mr. and Mrs. suddenly fall away.

The next group of babies listed are presented as the progeny of parents who do not merit the titles of Mr. and Mrs. The casual reader might have assumed that a printer's error had occurred; it would be corrected in tomorrow's edition of the *Gazette.* The more astute observer of the social scene would know in a flash that those infants, whose parents were recorded by first name only, were black kids. My entry begins, "William and Margaret Roberts, son Terrence."

In his book *The Birth and Death of Meaning*, cultural anthropologist Ernest Becker writes: "It is the task of culture to provide each and every single individual with the firm conviction that he or she is an object of primary value in a world of meaningful action." That was not the case for me. Prevailing cultural mores, held firmly upright by a supportive legal system, decreed that, as a black child, I did not count. I would not be deemed a person of value by any stretch of the imagination. I could erase all thoughts about being involved in any meaningful way in the action and passion of my times.

Frankly, I concluded as a very young person that Little Rock must be some kind of aberration. That outside the geographical confines of this city, people of sanity and reason lived in harmony and unity with each other. Such naïve speculation on my part was abolished as I became more ambulatory. My forays into regions other than Little Rock confirmed a truth that had been lurking in the back of my mind: This entire nation was filled with crazy people! But, in fact, there were no signs of ongoing mental illness.

There was, however, a penchant for making decisions predicated on things racial. Any and all exchanges, interactions, distributions of goods and services, or permissions to participate at all levels of society had a racial component. Where one could live, work, go to school; where one could shop; who one could marry; who could qualify for a bank loan—all of these possibilities were screened through a racial lens, and blackness was always a limiting factor. Whiteness was revered and seemed to outweigh any other asset in the contest for society's prizes.

In the midst of such craziness, it would not be unusual for one left out of the center of action to give up on life, to sit by the side of the road and bemoan the sad state of affairs that had led to this predicament. But what is remarkable to me, and stands today as a monument to the powers of the human spirit, the message I received from black people in my family and community countermanded the script tossed to me by the larger society.

Black people in my life said no to the lies of white supremacy. They exposed the myth of white superiority, and demanded that I put forth maximum effort to live life at the fullest, to realize and to activate my own potential. "Boy, get your education," were words spoken to me at every turn. Even those who had no formal training at all delivered those same lines with a practiced ease.

In first grade, Ms. Waugh, a remarkable educator, said this: "You must become the executive in charge of your own education; you have to become the CEO of your own individual learning enterprise." She, and most other black adults in my life were not willing to meet us with minimal expectations. They knew the power inherent in affirming our right to be stars in this universe. In a way somewhat akin to the affirmative-action program promulgated by this country on behalf of white males, black people in Little Rock used their resources to propel us toward excellence. We saw the obvious contrasts, and in the light of that reality we internalized truth, and resisted the tug of the national narrative that would have us accept second-class citizenship; and we pledged allegiance to learning, growth and self-development.

And it is that part of my story that I want to emphasize today. By whatever road you have traveled, by whatever means you have employed, you are here today as proof of your commitment to higher education. Your choice to learn separates you from a very large cadre of your fellow human beings. As strange as it may sound, there seems to be some great resistance on the part of far too many to enlarge their storehouse of knowledge and information.

In truth, the largest possession you own is your storehouse of ignorance. The good news: this is not a permanent condition. Some of you already know this truth, and your tenure at this institution has been marked by a keen dedication to the process of learning. Others of you, for reasons that you alone could express, have not yet decided to use all of your resources in the service of diminishing the size of that useless impediment.

I challenge all of you to intensify your efforts to learn all that life has to teach you. For some of you, today's ceremony is yet another step along the way in your sojourn through formal educational systems; for others this represents a culmination of this particular kind of formalized education. Yet, for all of us assembled here today, learning continues apace.

You see, for me, education—in its truest sense—is knowing what options are available in the universe. And how many options are there? Billions! Yes, billions, and yet, none of us know very many of them.

For me, learning is one of the most exciting endeavors we could ever undertake. As a middle-school student, I walked around with a dictionary, so that I could quickly figure out what was being said in my surround. For my efforts I was accorded the status of "nerd" by my peers. And, I must say to you, I wore my "nerd hat" with pride!

Don't allow the opinions of others to determine your course of action. What other people think about you is none of your business. What you think of yourself is what matters most. And if you think that achieving a level of excellence in the use of language is a preferred option, then by all means keep the pages of your dictionary open.

Recently I gave a talk to a group of eight graders; they appeared to be bored and inattentive. I asked this question: "How many of you really want to be in school today?" No hands were raised in response. "How many of you would prefer…" and before I could even complete the question all of their hands were raised skyward. In response to their enthusiastic embrace of the possibility of being someplace other than school, I said this: "You are all cowards."

That got their attention. The protests were immediate and the excuses rampant. They blamed parents, teachers, school officials, truant officers, and the government for forcing them to go to school. I was adamant in my refusal to accept their perceptions, and referred once again to their cowardice. I learned very quickly that it was unreasonable for me to expect members of this age-group cohort to get the point of taking personal responsibility for their actions. They raced down to the principal's office, and yelled to him as they pointed back to me: "That guy Roberts says we don't have to be here!" They missed the point, entirely.

But I trust that same point is not lost on this audience. If you choose to be in school, at work, join a social group, become a spouse or a parent for that matter, be totally committed to the process. Life at its best is about learning how to be the best you can be. Don't settle for less. Don't allow others to make those vital decisions for you.

I know the importance of being accepted for the person you are—how vital it is for you to feel that you belong. Each time I stepped onto the campus of Gibbs Elementary School, Dunbar Junior High School, and Horace Mann High School, I knew without doubt that I was a loved individual. All of the adults and a majority of my fellow students were in my corner, urging me on to academic success. This changed for the absolute worst when I arrived at Central High School. No longer was there the warm, nurturing environment I had come to appreciate and depend upon in the all-black schools. At Central I was vilified, abused, physically attacked, and treated with disdain. But, as imperative as the nurturing environment may be, it is not impossible to succeed under adverse circumstances.

The Nine understood the reality of our predicament, and we were determined not to allow the circumstances to dictate outcomes for us. We took to heart my first grade teacher's admonition, and developed mechanisms to blunt the impact of the physical and psychological warfare waged against us. In my case, I created an internal rating scale for insults hurled in my direction. My interest was creative content: If an insult were deemed creative enough, I would have been willing to rate it as high as ten, the upper limit of my scale. A rating of one was indicative of a decided lack of creative ability. Nobody scored higher than two that year. Often I would think to myself, "That was the same kind of nigger you called me yesterday. Where is your creativity?"

We were nonviolent in our response to the provocations from the horde of oppositionists. Dr. Martin Luther King, Jr., had come to Little Rock to introduce the concept, and urged us to consider adopting nonviolence as a strategy. He told us that the only way it would work was if we could truthfully say that we loved our enemies. After some deliberation we all agreed that yes, we do love our enemies.

For me it was a matter of living out the Golden Rule: "Do unto others as you would have them do unto you." When I first heard that rule, I was overjoyed. Hallelujah, I said! Life is going to be grand. I am not going to do anything to anybody! The trouble with this position is readily seen: What if others don't abide by the same rule?

And, of course, such a situation prevailed at Central. Our antagonists saw us not as nonviolent resistors, but as stationary targets. As a way of responding to this dilemma, I followed the advice given by my compatriot Jefferson Thomas who said to me, "Terry, when they said turn the other cheek, they didn't say you had to stand there and turn it. You can run down to the other end of the hall and turn it there." Jeff's logic made sense to me!

Even under the most adverse circumstances, we can choose to learn. Your fifth-level commitment, your willingness to do whatever it takes, will sustain you in the face of perceived obstacles. You will, no doubt, be forced out of your comfort zone.

But count that as a valuable happenstance. If you continue to reside in the center of the cocoon you have spun for yourself, very little growth can occur. At times learning may be painful. It may become an unwitting catalytic agent in the dissolution of favored relationships when your learning transports you to places in the universe where those in your inner circle choose not to go. How you respond to these critical markers in time and space will speak clearly about your level of commitment to growth and development. "It was good enough for my father, it will be good enough for me," may not be the mantra you want to play on the continuous loop in your brain.

On the gravel-topped playground at Gibbs Elementary School, one of the students who shunned the mantle of learner for himself leaped onto my back, and sent me sprawling face down into the gravel. I have a hunch that he attacked me because he resented my positive attitude toward school, learning, and all that related to the process.

I was reminded of that long-ago incident last month as I addressed a group of high school students in Cleveland, Ohio. During the question and answer period, a young black male student stood up and said that my use of big words indicated that I had chosen to act as if I were white. He wanted to know why I had made such a choice. I was stunned, and for a few seconds I could not find words to respond. As I struggled to find an adequate reply, I noted scenes playing out like a rearview projection on the walls of my mind. One of those scenes showed me face down in the gravel on the Gibbs playground.

My recall of the actual response I gave to the young man in Cleveland is somewhat hazy. I must have reminded him that learning, and the use of language, cannot be color-coded; that there is no such thing as "acting white." I may have reminded him as well that all people come equipped with potential to be developed. Or, I may even have added that history did not support his implied assumption.

But, for me, the overwhelming emotion was despair. Even as I responded to his inquiry, I was wrestling with a feeling that the gulf between us was so huge that I could not be assured that he even heard me. The idiocy of his assumption is patently obvious, but apparently not to him or to those for whom he may stand as a living symbol. It is, unfortunately, a testament to the lasting power of racist ideology. Binding a man's mind is more effective by far than binding his limbs with chains.

Finally, your task as you go forth from this place, includes an understanding of and an agreement to engage in repair of the world. In *The Prophet*, Gibran writes: "Like a procession you walk together towards your god-self. You are the way and the wayfarers. And when one of you falls down, he falls for those behind him, a caution against the stumbling stone. Ay, and he falls for those ahead of him, who though faster and surer of foot, yet removed not the stumbling stone."

From the Jewish tradition comes the concept of Tikkun Olam, an admonition to work toward repair of the world. It is important that you know that such a task can never be completed; but you are not released from your commitment to do all you can to make it happen. Make it your business to create a world wherein all people can freely embrace the process of learning; where artificial barriers are destroyed, and where any and all who want to choose excellence as a way of life can do so without feeling the wrath from others who would seek to color-code the universe.

Choosing to Lead an Ethical Life

Graduation speech at Westridge Academy

Friday, June 9, 2006

Any investigation of ethics is likely to focus attention on the principles of conduct governing individual or group behavior. And, in turn, those principles will prove to be based upon a set of values intrinsic to the society in which the individual or group claims membership.

Immediately we see a dilemma: There is a palpable difference between professed values and ensuing action. In some circles this is referred to as the value/ethics gap. In our recent history we have seen the gap widen to proportions that threaten our sense of well-being.

In some communities there is an aura of disbelief, a refusal to even entertain the thought that leaders in education, health care, government, business, and industry could stray so far from the values we cherish. At the other end of the continuum there are those who express a lack of trust in all those who occupy positions of leadership and authority. In every sector, questions abound about levels of honesty, integrity, fairness, virtue, character, and moral courage.

Finally, we are forced to admit that nothing has really changed. The value/ethics gap is not a new phenomenon suddenly sprung into existence. At all times and in all ages, it has been evident that some of us have more difficulty than others maintaining a reasonable balance between what we profess and what we do. In fact, many take the position that since we seem to be doomed to lead imperfect lives anyway, why strive to do what is right or just? Why not accept the human condition as one in which we will never be able to live up to the value standard we have adopted? The philosopher Thomas Hobbes gave voice to this sentiment when he averred that mankind is naturally selfish, implying that value standards would always be subjugated to personal desires and wishes. And it is with this backdrop that we face the question: What are the benefits of leading an ethical life?

A few months after I had moved to Los Angeles, California, in the late '50s, I saw a news report about an armored car that had lost a bag of money. The rear door had somehow opened during transit, and a bag containing $250,000 had fallen into the street. The money was mostly in small bills, and was being taken to the Treasury Department for eventual destruction because it had been in circulation for such a long time. Two days later, another news story reported that a man had come forward with the bag of money and turned it in to the authorities. He had found the bag and was frightened initially when he saw how much money was inside. Although he had briefly considered keeping the money, he decided the best course of action was an honest one. And for his honesty, he was given a $10,000 reward.

But, in contrast to the praise he received from the armored car company, he was vilified by members of his own family and by outspoken community members who chastised him, and said that he was a fool for giving the money back. Their position was based on the logic that the company could well afford to lose the money since they were insured; and besides, they were part of big business and would not hesitate to cheat the little guy; and since he was an ethnic minority person, he was owed the money anyway!

Under this barrage, his life fell apart: his wife divorced him, the Internal Revenue Service came looking for delinquent taxes on the $10,000, and he lost his job.

In this example, it is clear that penalties sometimes accrue in the wake of one's ethical decision. Not that his decision itself caused the series of traumatic events in his life, but it was the trigger for the responses to him. His choice to abide by principles of honesty did not endear him to those who would alter the standard of honesty to make it fit a personal-needs agenda.

A question we must ask is this: "In what ways have I compromised principle for the sake of personal gain?" This is not a question for idle musing, but one that can lead us to knowing more about self, and what drives us forward in this universe.

Would you have given the money back? High-level self-awareness is imperative in any discussion of ethical behavior. In fact, I have concluded that such understanding of self is the first step in any program designed to promote continuous ethical behavior.

And what do I mean by this? Just that you can know in advance what your response will be to any given situation; that you can know your intentions at any point of choice; that you can be intimately acquainted with the reasons why you do whatever you do in life. A large order, to be sure. But one that serves as a beacon to guide us through the labyrinths and mazes of life. We need some directional signals, some guideposts, and self-awareness is one of the best we can find.

There are, of course, some assumptions here. One of which is that you have learned to be honest with self, and you will listen to directives from within. Also, that the information you have used to help you develop this awareness is free from bias and contamination. Or, perhaps I should say, that the information has been sifted to eliminate all possible contaminants before it has been adopted for use. And again, I know that this calls for extremely diligent work. Much discipline and focus is necessary if one is to complete this arduous task. Yet, it can, and must, be done.

The next step is making a commitment to *use* the awareness in the service of growth and development. Having the awareness, with no commitment to use, is tantamount to not having it at all. And it is vital to know that various levels of commitment exist. The first four levels are highly suspect, but the fifth level makes sense.

The first four are arranged in this fashion: I'll think about it, I'll try, I'll do what I can, and I'll do what's expected. The fifth level: I'll do whatever it takes.

The fifth level is the only one that makes sense to me. One caveat here: Fifth-level commitment does not mean that you throw your body beneath the wheels of a speeding train. No. At times you will be called upon to retreat from the fray for a time of reflection and preparation, a time of contemplation and planning. Balance is the key word—a seeking of balance so that you can respond effectively to the challenges and requirements ahead of you.

Following your decision to make a fifth-level commitment, you can begin to look for the options best suited to your needs. This is the third step. And how many options are there? Billions!! But you don't know what they are because, like me, your largest single possession is a storehouse of ignorance. But rather than have this piece of information lead you into despair, use it as motivation to learn.

And finally, step four: Put into action whatever you choose at step three, fully aware that what you choose probably will not work. You see, the process of learning is such that time is required for you to find the set of choices that work best for you.

Using this four-step process can help bring clarity to ethical dilemmas you might face, especially when you enter the workplace. Consider this example: An administrator at a large university comes to the office on a Monday morning to be welcomed by an urgent message from a faculty member who explains that there is a problem concerning a recent donation to the scholarship fund. It seems that the monies were given with the stipulation that they be awarded to the student in the graduating class with the highest grade point average. The committee assigned to monitor this process has determined to award the scholarship to a student whose grade point average is not the highest, because the members felt the donor would be offended by the fact that the student with the highest average is a student of color. The student chosen by the committee is a white student, whose actual grade point average is several points lower than that of the top student. Most members of the committee felt that they wanted to insure continued donations from this donor, and did not want to do anything that might jeopardize that reality. The faculty member who alerts you to the situation feels opposed to the committee decision, and wants you to intervene and reverse the committee vote.

As the administrator, your job is to do what? What is the ethical dilemma being faced in this instance? And how does one use the four-step process? Obviously, this is not a problem that can be resolved with ease and simplicity. But, even so, high-level self-awareness is a necessary first step.

The administrator needs to know without doubt where he or she stands on the salient points. Will the main focus be on mollifying the donor on the assumption that he or she will be offended by a deserving student's racial group membership? Will attention be given to the committee's decision-making process? Will the administrator usurp the committee's role?

In fact, long lists of questions come to mind; but, in truth, the administrator can know all the answers in a flash if self-awareness exists in abundance. And I realize this is a big if; developing true self-awareness is a lifelong activity. Yet, by leaning in that direction, a working self-awareness can yield effective and useful results.

The next step, that of commitment, follows immediately. Having or making a fifth-level commitment means that whatever is required will be done. And this, of course, opens the door to all the available options.

That leaves the final step, action. And it is this final step that all players in this scenario await, because the administrator has the last word. As the administrator in this vignette, what would you have done?

Making informed choices in the face of ethical dilemmas is an ongoing challenge. Beyond knowing self, the competent administrator must know as much as possible about the motives and expectations of others. Why? Because everything done by humans is done in the context of relationship with others.

As we plan a life of ethical action, we necessarily have to factor in the nature of all the relationships we have with those around us. For instance, do we break the rules for our friends? Do we make allowances for some but not for others?

I am reminded here of my late professor and colleague, Harry Kitano. He once said to me that he had spent the maximum amount of time at all levels of the academic trek toward full professorship. His journey up the ladder was in stark contrast to others who often spent only the minimum amount of time at each level. The prevailing question, of course, would be, how were the determinations made? Who decided that one professor would leap ahead, while another must grind away in the trenches until deemed ready to advance? Obviously in cases such as this, we would have to look very carefully at the process by which tenure was awarded in each instance. But, we could not make the mistake of assuming anything at all; the whole procedure would have to be investigated.

I say this because some years ago, I was selected to sit on an academic review committee to investigate a complaint from an adjunct professor. In his allegation, the professor contended that he had been terminated without just cause; that he had been an adjunct for twenty years and had never had a bad review. His termination letter stated that he was simply not performing up to standard. The professor said that it was simply a personality clash between him and the new department chair.

The chairperson of the academic review committee started our first meeting with these words: "We have to assume that the University acted in good faith." I went ballistic at that point. Admittedly, my behavior was not conducive to clear, objective exchange, but I was horrified to think that the process would be so skewed at the beginning. In my estimation, it was the job of our committee to determine who had acted in good faith or, for that matter, who had acted in bad faith. We were charged with finding the facts, and submitting our findings. The committee chairperson was not acting ethically as I saw it. He saw it differently. And this is not, unfortunately, an atypical situation. We reconvened and completed our work, but on a more objective basis.

Choosing to lead an ethical life demands that one also lead a life of responsibility: a life in which one is willing to be held accountable for decisions made; a life where one is capable of fulfilling an obligation; a life of trustworthiness.

In closing, I will share with you an allegory that illustrates some of the points I have tried to make here:

The geese children were flying as they had always flown. In their V formation, they swooped across the sky, giving loud voice to their sheer delight in being together. The spirit of the sky saw them and was disturbed, because he noted the inefficiency of their formation. In his mind it would be better if they flew in single file. And so, with that thought in mind, the spirit of the sky came down to confront the geese children.

"You are inefficient," he said. "From now on I want you to fly in single file. Who is your leader? I want to speak to him myself."

The geese children protested and said that they had always flown in V formations. They said also that there was no single leader; that they all took turns, and whoever was feeling strongest on a given day was the leader. Further, they pleaded, "We can look out for each other when we are in the V formation."

But the spirit of the sky was not dissuaded. He demanded that they pick a leader and fly in single file. The geese children were stymied by this, and simply could not wrap their minds around the idea of choosing a single leader. The spirit of the sky, in utter frustration and disgust, transformed himself into a large goose, and became, by fiat, the leader of the geese children.

Under his tutelage they learned to fly in single file. After a time they came to believe that this was a better way after all. The spirit of the sky praised them for finally coming to their senses.

As they flew off, an eagle hovered overhead, and noticed that the geese children were flying in single file. Almost beside himself with glee at this unexpected good fortune, the eagle took the last goose in line for his evening meal. The other geese, flying in single file and looking straight ahead, were unaware of the eagle's attack.

Word spread quickly throughout the kingdom of eagles, and each last-in-line goose was picked off by a hungry bird of prey. When the spirit of the sky decided to stop for the night, he was shocked to find that all of the geese children had disappeared. Meanwhile, the creator had noticed the drama unfolding below him, and his anger was apparent. He confronted the spirit of the sky and asked him what had happened to his geese children. The spirit of the sky said, "It was not my fault. It was those eagles!"

And finally, leading an ethical life means taking into consideration that we share this planet with all others. Together we make up one large community. We have responsibility for self, yes; but also we have responsibility for each other. The great educator Horace Mann gave us these words: "Be ashamed to die until you have won some victory for humanity."

Lessons from Little Rock[2]

Talk presented at Huntington Library

March 29, 2006

It was an inauspicious start to say the least, having been born in Little Rock, Arkansas, into a society that did not welcome my arrival. I came into the world clothed in the regal robes of blackness only to find that the color of the day was white; white skin was the preferred dermatological covering. Whiteness reigned supreme in every corner of what was euphemistically called the civilized world. This fact was prominently displayed wherever and whenever possible. It was on view whenever one would see the signs over public toilet facilities: MEN – WOMEN – COLORED, not even the distinction of gender for the latter group. In places of business, in governmental buildings, in churches, in sports arenas, in fact, wherever people might gather, there were visible lines of separation by racial group membership. Black people were reminded at every turn that they were not members of society's inner circle; that they were, in fact, very far removed from any meaningful part of life in the wider community.

My education about life in America continued apace as I grew, learned more about life, and ventured out into the environs of greater Little Rock. It wasn't long before I was well schooled in the art of survival in this hostile territory; and believe me, such knowledge was invaluable, absolutely necessary, and not always easy to come by. Fortunately for me there were black people around who were willing to help me figure out the nuances of racism, the subtleties of discriminatory behavior. I could see for myself the most salient overt racist actions and the obvious rejections, but I still needed expertise in handling the "wolves in sheep's clothing."

Oh, it was, at first, very puzzling indeed; but I was a quick learner. Eventually, I was able to master the art of dealing with racism in all its variations. Yet, the whole thing was so irrational and unreasonable that at times I despaired and wondered what the future might hold for me. At one point I remember thinking that Little Rock must be an aberration; that elsewhere in the United States people must have learned how to co-exist without the racial prejudices so prevalent around me. This was all magnified by the fact that I was a very rational thinker; I demanded to know how such a legal and social reality could have been allowed to develop. The answers were unsatisfactory. I was more often than not advised to keep my voice down, don't make a fuss, it's the law of the land. None of these answers made sense to me, and I wanted to find the rational basis for what I saw happening around me. It was simply not to be. In one sense I shared a kinship with the poet Countee Cullen who wrote the poem "Yet Do I Marvel" in 1925. His poem reads as follows:

"I doubt not God is good, well-meaning, kind,
And did He stoop to quibble could tell why
The little buried mole continues blind,
Why flesh that mirrors Him must someday die,
Make plain the reason tortured Tantalus
Is baited by the fickle fruit, declare
If merely brute caprice dooms Sisyphus
To struggle up a never-ending stair.
Inscrutable His ways are, and immune
To catechism by a mind too strewn
With petty cares to slightly understand
What awful brain compels His awful hand.
Yet do I marvel at this curious thing:
To make a poet black, and bid him sing!

I would ask the question, why make me such a rational being and expect me to live in such an irrational world? This question and others like it helped to stimulate my desire to learn as much as I possibly could about how to change the world around me. And eventually that commitment led me to join the group now known as the Little Rock Nine. It was not a linear journey by any means; but the twists and turns were, in retrospect, designed to lead me to the realization that this opportunity was not to be missed. The window was open slightly, but not very wide, and might not remain open for very long. So, I volunteered, me and a host of others numbering around 150, if my memory is correct. That number dwindled, as you well know, to a single digit—primarily a function of winnowing by the school authorities as they sought a cadre of good students and good citizens, plus acts of protection on the part of fearful parents. With the governor himself speaking loudly in public about armed caravans coming to town to prevent integration, and with armed thugs already roaming the streets of Little Rock, it is easy to see how some parents would find it hard to give their children permission to be involved in this dangerous experimental venture.

But, the group of nine remaining shared a belief that life under the prevailing conditions was no life at all, really. We were willing to face the opposition, stand up for the principles of right, act according to the spirit of justice and equality often spoken about but rarely seen when black people were included in the equation. Even so, with all of our readiness to take on this assignment, with our unwavering conviction, and our hope for a brighter future, we were frightened beyond belief.

I had never been so afraid in my life. Fear was not only a constant companion but a daily reminder that we could be killed at any time. This was not a random fear, but one based in stark, deadly reality. Threats were everywhere: in the loud voices of the mobs surrounding Central High School and roaming around the near vicinity of the school; in the snarling voices on our home telephones at all hours of the night and day; in the pages of hate mail that arrived each weekday and Saturday with the regular postal delivery. I have a telegram that I have yet to assign to either the category of support or to the stack of hate mail that I collected. The telegram reads: "We will never forget what you did here," signed, a white lady. I suppose since she identified herself as a lady I should lean toward putting her missive in the support pile; but, you never know!

Most of you know that we were only able to enter the school with the help of the United States Army, specifically the 101st Airborne Division, a unit famous for showing up in places where much trouble is expected. And trouble is what they found when they arrived. The citizens of Little Rock, led by the governor, loudly protested the presence of the 101st. Members of the Capital Citizens Council, the Ku Klux Klan, the White Citizens Association, and assorted independent racists railed against the army unit. In an effort to appease these folk the unit commander, General Edwin Walker, ordered his troops, all white by the way, to maintain as low a profile as possible. What this meant in practice was that soldiers could escort us to the door of our classrooms but they could not enter; they could take us to the entrance to the gymnasium but they had to stay outside; they could not go into the bathrooms, the library, the cafeteria or the school auditorium. What this meant also was that we were obviously more vulnerable to attacks in those areas where the soldiers were forbidden to go.

This was especially true for me in the gymnasium where PE classes were held. I was a target for all manner of mayhem in that environment. It was in the gym where my personal antagonist could dream up ever new ways to torment me. Jerry Tuley was good at his job. It was as if he had trained at summer camp or someplace to learn how to make life miserable for me. He taunted, punched, and kicked me in the hallways and in the homeroom we shared; but it was in PE where he displayed his full range of hateful actions toward me. It was in the gym one day when the coach called for all of us to stand in a semicircle around him, and he addressed the issue of what he had seen happening.

"You boys are always sneaking up behind Roberts (he called us all by last name) and doing things to him; but you know what, I think you are a bunch of cowards. Yes, cowards, because if you were truly men, you wouldn't sneak up behind him; you would walk up to him face-to-face and challenge him to the mat." And with that he pointed to the wrestling mat so that nobody would misunderstand his intent.

Now this was a huge surprise for me! This was not something the coach and I had worked out in advance. No, this was his way of introducing fair play and teaching us manly behavior. What I concluded was that I would probably die that morning in the gym. Tuley and all the rest of them lined up to take me on, and they had looks of sheer hatred plastered on their faces, which were twisted and distorted to amplify the looks of hatred. I would demonstrate that tortured look if I could, but I simply don't know how human beings manage to abuse their faces in that manner.

I looked at Tuley, who had assumed first position in line, and said to myself, "Jerry Tuley, you are so anxious to be wherever I am, you should know that I am just about to depart this universe, and for you to follow me, you must leave also." And, since I was the only one who understood this rather bizarre dynamic, I would have to be the one to ensure his demise. In a rare state of near absolute calm, I went to the mat with Jerry, with the thought of his death on my mind.

He had worn a set of military dog tags to school that day, and as I threw him down with a vicious headlock, I grabbed the chain around his neck and used it as an instrument to restrict his air supply. Almost instantly he began to turn blue and gasp for air. Seeing this play out, the coach ran over and broke it up. "Get out of here!" he shouted. "Get out of the gym, all of you." With his voice of disgust shooing us outside, we all filed out onto the playing field; and even as we made our way out while the coach remained inside, I knew something else was awaiting me.

It didn't take very long for the "something else" to show up. Suddenly, without a lot of fanfare, I found myself surrounded by my classmates. I was in the center of a large circle, and I looked at the array of twisted faces to see if I could figure out what was to come. It came soon enough, in the form of McCauley, a senior at Central that year and one of the largest students in the school. He was a football player and a member of the Naval Reserve. This information, along with his picture, was readily available in the school student directory, so I knew who he was right away. He came stalking toward me with the determination of a man on a mission. He held a baseball bat in his right hand, swinging it lightly back and forth as he approached.

There was no way I could even imagine taking him on, since he was literally three times my size. What I did was to make eye contact with him, and held that gaze as he came nearer. And he came as close as he could. We stood there nose to nose, breathing on each other for what seemed to be an eternity. Finally, he spoke for the first time: "Nigger, if you weren't so small..." And his voice trailed off. He dropped the bat and walked away. Macauley had discovered a spark of humanity hidden deeply within himself, a spark even he could not override. He could not force himself to take undue advantage of a smaller human being.

Needless to say, that was a moment filled with more drama than I needed. For an uncertain moment I was on the verge of becoming the subject of a coroner's report. A second or two later, I was standing petrified and paralyzed with fear as my would-be attacker and his cohorts slowly dispersed and walked away, mumbling and grumbling to themselves. My state of fear was so profound that for several minutes I doubted my capacity to walk upright, even if I could convince my body that it was indeed prudent to leave the spot where I was seemingly glued to the turf. Eventually I summoned the energy to ambulate, and made my way toward the gym where I knew yet another ordeal awaited me.

The school rules were clearly stated, well-known by all students, and enforced with vigor by the keepers of high-school decorum at Central High. Students had to shower each day after gym class, no exceptions. For me this entailed having to cope with extremely hot water pouring from all of the shower heads which were, invariably, pointed in my direction, and to step gingerly around the broken glass scattered randomly on the shower floor. Suffice it to say, all my showers that year were lightning fast. This day was no exception.

As I made my way toward the lockers, however, I made what could have been a fatal mistake. I forgot to maintain high-level vigilance. I approached my locker with one thought: spin the numbers, open the locker, and get dressed. I did not see several students approaching me from behind, and one of them threw a combination lock with great force and accuracy. I was struck on the head so hard I thought I might pass out. Falling to one knee, I heard the scuffle of feet running toward me, and I figured out what was happening. I knew if I didn't get up quickly I would have more than a sore head to deal with.

Finding a bit of leverage by leaning against the bank of lockers, I lurched forward toward the threshold of the coach's office which, fortunately, was nearby. He was at his desk, looked up and saw that I was bleeding from the head wound, soaking wet, totally naked. He leaped up without a word to me, and ran out to see if he could intercept the ones who had thrown the lock. They had disappeared by then, so the coach assisted me with first aid after I had dried off; and finally I opened the locker only to be confronted by cascading water. Somebody had filled the locker up to the air vents, and all of my clothing was soaking wet.

This presented a true dilemma, since I knew immediately that I would have to make a phone call home and have my mom bring a change of clothing. But, the one thing I did not want to do at any time that year was to make a phone call home in the middle of the day. Why? Because even though my mom and I had not discussed this at all, I knew that she hovered over the phone all day, answering each time it rang before the first ring was complete. She did not want to miss the call that informed her that her son was no longer among the living. After some initial hesitation, however, I made the call; she brought the necessary change of clothing and we both returned to the rest of that day's agenda.

It was twenty years later when my mom and I were having lunch in Los Angeles—where we had moved in 1958 following the closure of Little Rock's high schools—that those scenes from the gym came roaring back to my conscious awareness. As we ate lunch that day, my mom asked me what seemed to be a rather odd question. "Terry," she said, "do you remember that high school you attended in Little Rock?" "Well," she continued, "one day I got a phone call, and the man on the other end of the line said in a rather official voice, 'I am sorry to have to inform you, but your son, Terrence, has been savagely beaten; I don't know if he will survive for another hour. He was beaten with a tire iron, and he has several broken bones.'"

You can just about imagine what happened to my mom as she heard those words. Here was the call she had dreaded. In a state of panic and near hysteria, she made her way up to the school. The principal helped to calm her down, and escorted her to my classroom where she looked in and saw that I was okay; nothing had happened. But the psychological damage had been done.

As she related this story I could feel chill bumps going up and down my spine. I realized as I sat there that I had no idea about the true psychological cost paid by my parents. They were truly remarkable people whose sole purpose in all of that madness was to keep me as safe as possible; and that meant, in part, concealing a great deal of ugliness.

The lessons from Little Rock have been amplified over time, and remain salient for me in these opening years of the 21st Century. I learned that people do what they wish to do when they have the power to do so. This may seem somewhat simplistic, but nonetheless, it is an important lesson to consider. The citizens of Little Rock did not want to integrate Central High School, and they made their wishes known through organized, violent opposition.

A few years after the chaos at Central, I had an opportunity to meet Governor Faubus, whose erstwhile leadership in Little Rock nearly led to the death of the nine of us, simply because we wanted to attend a neighborhood school. We were backstage on the set of "Good Morning America," a television show where both of us had been invited to discuss the integration of Central High; and I confronted the governor and asked why he had endangered our lives. His response was that if he had not acted as he did, he might have been voted out of office for failing to follow the will of the people. And so you see, the lesson pertains: the people wanted segregation, Faubus wanted to remain in office, and the power of law and custom was on their side.

Another very salient lesson is that you cannot color-code racism. Not every single white person in Little Rock was my enemy, nor was every single black person my friend. On that first day of school when we were barred from entry by the Arkansas State National Guardsmen, I was followed home by a white man who simply wanted to say that he did not support segregation, and that he wished things were different. On the other hand my neighbor, a black woman, wanted to know why I was causing so much trouble.

Racism is a way of thinking that can be adopted by anyone who wishes to place whiteness at the top of a hierarchy designed to order people by the degree to which they approximate the ideals of whiteness. As we look around us, we see that the voices in support of the status quo are not coming solely from those who hold membership in the so-called white race.

In 1998 I was hired by the Little Rock School District as a desegregation consultant. In the four years that I worked for them, I had opportunity to interact with a rather large number of my former white classmates at Central High who were now employed by the school district. And yet, almost to a person, they said to me, "I didn't do it; I was not one of the ones beating you up in 1957."

So what is the lesson to be learned? People will rewrite history when it is convenient to do so. Although, I must say, there was one man who confessed to a different crime from that era. He saw me in the Little Rock airport and introduced himself as one of my PE classmates. I literally took a step or two backwards when he said this, remembering all of the pain and misery I had endured in that class. He quickly assured me he was not one of the antagonists, but he did confess to being a silent onlooker. He apologized for not coming to my defense in 1957, and stated further that he had suffered emotionally since that time for what he perceived to be an act of cowardice on his part. The lesson is obvious here: When one does not follow the dictates of conscience, one possible consequence may be mental and emotional turmoil.

But, in truth, mental and emotional anguish may not be totally avoided, even when one acts according to higher moral principles. One of my former classmates at Central was Hazel Bryant, self-described as having been the poster child for American racism in 1957. She was bad. Her twisted countenance was captured by photographer Will Counts in his celebrated photo of Elizabeth Eckford, one of the Little Rock Nine, as she was subjected to the verbal abuse of Hazel and her counterparts when Elizabeth arrived unescorted on the first day of school, when we were turned away by the National Guard.

On one of my trips to Little Rock in my role as consultant to the school district, Hazel telephoned me and we met for lunch. I knew by then that she had decided to give up racist thinking and action, and she wanted to personally apologize for her behavior in 1957. She told me that when she gave birth to her own children, it dawned on her that she did not want to raise them as racists. And, because she made that choice, she was kicked out of her family of origin. She is now persona non grata in that continuing stronghold of racist thought and action. She is being forced to deal with the emotional residue accumulated in the wake of that reality.

Another one of my former classmates, Robin Woods, did choose to act according to higher principles during the chaotic year at Central High. She pulled her desk close to mine in

Algebra class one day so we could share her book. More often than not, my books and supplies were destroyed by hostile classmates who were determined to do anything possible to make my life at Central as bad as it could be. Robin had grown up in a household with parents who preached the gospel of inclusion, who told her that all people were to be treated as fellow human beings, so her spontaneous act in algebra class was not at all unusual.

What made Robin's experience different was that sometimes children grow up in homes where they hear the same words Robin heard, but there is no real support for those sentiments. What they hear is empty rhetoric. In those homes, when kids act on the things they have heard, parents are often incensed and then confront the kids with the real messages they want to convey. Fortunately, in Robin's case, the parental injunctions were congruent with actions taken by her parents; there was no hidden agenda. But even so, Robin, who lives in Little Rock today, has emotional pain because she sees far too many of her peers who continue to harbor racist ideology.

Another very pertinent lesson for me was that not all of those who profess Christian beliefs support the notion of inclusion. It had always been my assumption that Christianity was based, at least in part, on treating all others with dignity and respect. This was simply not true in Little Rock. Many of the white people in the Monday morning mobs at Central had spent the greater part of Sunday in prayer and worship at the local churches. And in yet another twist on this theme, a black minister said to me, "You know you have no business up there at that school; but since you are there, you might as well stay." I would have sworn it was the business of Christians to be on the front lines of the fight for social justice, by choice, and not simply because of happenstance!

Yes, the lessons abound, and they remain pertinent for us in this year, 2006. We have the power to eliminate racism, but we lack the will. We have the ability to practice inclusion, but we seem to prefer exclusion. Our willingness to challenge the status quo pales beside our vigorous support of business as usual. We are surprised by the living conditions unveiled in the aftermath of Katrina, but that surprise gives way all too soon to our preferred focus on who shall remain on the island, or who shall be crowned the year's American idol.

On the last page of his book, *Defending the Spirit: A Black Life in America,* Randall Robinson writes these words:

"...If I have appeared angry, that anger in all likelihood understates the well-masked temper of blacks generally. I don't know what Asians or Hispanics think because I know no Asians or Hispanics well enough. This is intrinsic to the problem. We are, in America, now sealed off from each other in well-defended racial camps with negligible inter-group knowledge or communication. Our nation's white leaders have elected, consciously or unconsciously, to ignore the deepening national racial crisis. In so doing, they have set us all on a course toward disaster."

Robinson's text was published in 1998, and his voice by far is not the lone cry in the wilderness. Others speak the same truth; but, because what they have to say is not congruent with the national narrative that tells us we already have solved the racial issues in this country, their voices are muted.

Some attempt to subvert the dialogue by contending that the real issue is not race, but class. The truth is we cannot separate and dichotomize any of these ascribed attributes. It is at their confluence that we have to study and analyze the true impact of what it means to be so defined.

For me, this quest for understanding started in Little Rock, and continues as I try to ferret out the ways in which I can traverse this terrain with some degree of certainty that real change is possible. That America will, at some point, live up to the ideals so prominently displayed in the articles of governance, in the Constitutional rhetoric, in the public pronouncements of those who have been elected to serve in our houses of government, and which are displayed, in part, on the very coin of the realm we use for daily commerce. I trust this has not been a futile quest, one that will end in frustration and despair; for I doubt I can look into the eyes of my grandsons, Paul Jr. and Austin, and feel good about their prospects for life in this country if that is the case.

There is no reason for any of this to have ever been. Yet, in the spirit of accepting the reality of our existence, I say our task now is to find the least detrimental available alternative to the mess we have made. It is my plan to be guided by the lessons from Little Rock as I seek to find those alternatives, and I urge you to join me. Together we can create a space called America that has little resemblance to this rather stagnant pond we sometimes so blithely refer to as the mainstream.

And, as I close these remarks, I am reminded of the words of yet another poet, Langston Hughes:

We have tomorrow
Bright before us
Like a flame.

Yesterday
A night-gone thing,
A sun-down name.

And dawn-today
Broad arch above
the road we came.

We march!

Reflections on Life in Little Rock

Riall Lecture

Salisbury University
Salisbury, Maryland

Presented on April 3, 2007

It is an honor for me to have been chosen to give the Riall lecture this academic year. The roll call of those who have preceded me speak in stentorian tones that I am indeed in the midst of select company.

Tonight, as I begin, I bring you greetings from the other eight members of the Little Rock Nine. As we plan ceremonies and sponsor gatherings in this fiftieth year since the chaos of 1957, we recognize that many of you present in this auditorium offered prayers on our behalf, and shared the anxiety and fear that we carried with us to school each day. For that we thank you, and ask, in our own prayers, that God smile upon you always.

Although at this juncture in space and time it seems impossible to even conceive, for a very long time this country, our country, was convinced that separating groups of people on the basis of racial-group membership was the legal, moral, expected, desirable, and constitutional thing to do. In fact, if we were to start a timeline in 1619 and extend it without interruption to the year 1954, we would see in stark, graphic reality a period of 335 years during which time the United States of America used its considerable powers and resources to build and maintain walls of separation between the designated groups. This way of life was underscored in 1896 when the Supreme Court ruled in the Plessy case that discrimination was constitutional. Such a ruling was necessary because the challenges to the status quo were mounting, and the Court wanted no ambiguity to cloud the thinking of American citizens.

In truth, oppressed groups were not sitting idly by as the 335-year period progressed; challenges were ever in the offing, usually to no avail. One of my favorite cases can be found in the archives under its legal identification, Roberts v. City of Boston, 1849. I like this one primarily because of the surname of the plaintiff. Roberts lost his appeal to the Massachusetts State Supreme Court, but he had fought long and hard to enroll his children in the Boston public schools. But his kids were black, and that one fact was enough to keep them out of the halls of education. It was a series of legal protests against the apartheid of the day that led to the 1954 ruling in the Brown case that declared racial discrimination to be no longer constitutional.

Since the legal demise of discrimination, we have enjoyed 53 years of existence. As you juxtapose the two time periods, 335 years to 53 years, you see readily the great imbalance, the skewed picture we have created. And, you realize at a glance that 1954 was not a stopping point; it was simply a new starting point. The line started in 1619 continues, fading somewhat with each new generation; the line started in 1954 moves ahead, becoming bolder, more meaningful with each new generation, or so some of us surmise in our more hopeful musings. There are days, however, when it seems that the residual carryover, the leakage, the institutionalized elements of the 335-year period threaten to erase the new line; to invalidate the markings etched into our psyche since 1954.

We enter the universe and step into a drama already underway. We have no hand in writing the script, but we have assigned roles to play. The unfortunate reality is that too many of us never question the roles we are given. We accept the validity of the plot as it moves toward its expected denouement. We accept at face value the validity of the interactions between the players.

I did question my assignment. It seemed odd that I was given a minor role, a subordinate part that left me out of the main cast. I was required to wait patiently in the wings for my cue to enter; and even when I was called forth, my part was so minimal that it seemed irrelevant to the overall dynamic taking place around me. As a young black male in Little Rock I was expected to learn the rules of segregation and follow them without comment. And in truth, I did follow the rules; but as I said, I questioned why I had to do so. My questioning was seen by the black adults in my life as potentially disruptive, and I was admonished to keep quiet, not to rock the boat, to keep my voice down, not to stir up trouble. Stir up trouble? I would wonder, trouble for whom? It seemed clear to me that we were in fairly serious trouble already! I didn't think the situation could get much worse. Of course that was from the vantage point of an untutored young black boy, new to the universe and confused beyond belief.

It was this confusion that eventually led me to do my own research in an attempt to make sense out of what was happening around me. I pondered the situation for a long time, and finally, when I was about nine years old, I came to a conclusion: white people are crazy. This seemed to make sense. They were in charge, and the system put in place was as crazy as I had ever seen. But, further reflection suggested that mental illness was not present to the degree necessary for what I was witnessing.

There was, however, a penchant for decision-making based on racial elements. All decisions in our society had a racial component. Where you could live, where you could work, whether you could buy property and where this property could be located, who you could marry, whether you could qualify for bank loans, where you could go to school—all these decisions and many others were tied directly to racial-group membership. Mental illness had to be ruled out, but I needed to know much more about this skewed system.

The Crystal Burger was a white-owned establishment in the city of Little Rock. It had the distinction of allowing black people to enter the front door to order food to go. We could not sit down to eat inside the Crystal Burger. That was one of the rules of segregation. This was one of my frequent haunts; I would stand there in the very circumscribed area designated for black people and order hamburgers, fries, and malts to go.

One summer day in my thirteenth year, I entered the Crystal Burger and made my usual order: burger, fries, and malt to go. But on this day, and I have no memory of what I must have been thinking at the time, I hopped up onto one of the stools in front of the counter to wait for my order to be prepared. This was a direct violation of the sacred code, and it was not viewed with favor by any of the white people in the Crystal Burger at that time. Proprietors and patrons alike all stopped whatever they had been doing and turned their attention to me. In a moment that seemed frozen very much akin to the static picture on the screen when someone pushes the pause button on a VCR, all the heads turned toward me.

The non-verbal message was clear as a bell: "Boy, you better get some sense in your head." Embarrassed beyond belief and angry to the nth degree, I left that place feeling as if I had been swatted away like one of the flies circling around inside the Crystal Burger. I cancelled my order that day, and never returned. After that episode, obeying the rules of segregation became arduous, difficult to the extreme, but the rules remained in place. My epiphany notwithstanding, I had no power to alter the situation.

It was, no doubt, my "coming of age" in the Crystal Burger that presaged my involvement with the group of nine who would enter Central High School. After that episode, I began to look for ways to ease the emotional pain I felt, now that my eyes were slightly more open; now that slights were seen in vivid color; now that words could no longer be ignored completely. There were few remedies for the things that gnawed at my gut.

In the wake of the Brown decision, the Little Rock School

Board decided to obey the law. There was absolutely no precedent for such an action. No way of explaining that a board comprised of white southerners would voluntarily begin plans to desegregate just because it was the lawful thing to do. They were good, I must say. Their first plan was brilliant, designed to succeed, and would most likely have done so but for the resistance of those who were appalled that the school board actually wanted this thing to work.

The initial plan called for desegregation at the kindergarten through third-grade levels. Try as hard as you might, it is difficult to conjure up images of race riots in kindergarten. The opposing forces were so determined, however, that they insisted that this very reasonable plan be scrapped in favor of one that contained maximum opportunity for chaos. Virgil Blossom, then Superintendent of Schools, felt that "...six year old children would be the least concerned about the color of the skin of classmates."

The compromise plan was grades 10 through 12 at one high school only, Central High. This plan was presented to the all-black student body at Horace Mann High School where I attended in the spring of 1957, and to ninth graders at the all-black Dunbar Junior High School. After listening to the parameters, about 150 of us volunteered to participate. Those numbers dwindled consistently for the next few months as a result of fear of violence, a very strict screening process developed by the school board, and concern about loss of jobs on the part of black parents.

Rumor has it that the school board was going to screen out 100% of the volunteers as a way of appeasing the more vocal and radical members of the opposition forces. Rumor further has it that Daisy Bates, president of the Arkansas State Chapter of the NAACP, called Blossom on this and he relented. I do know this: On the day before school was to begin, there were 10 of us. Jane Hill's father was contacted by his employer who told him that if Jane enrolled at Central, his job was history. He pulled his daughter out, and he lost his job anyway. A result I would have predicted if I had known about the situation. Jane's father had the temerity to think he could send her to Central. That was enough for the white employer; he would have no one working for him who thought he could be some kind of social equal.

Most of you know the story: We were kept out of school by the Arkansas National Guard, who had been called out by Governor Faubus; and it was not until Eisenhower sent in the 101st Airborne Division of the United States Army that we were granted admission. We languished outside school for three weeks as we awaited the outcome of the legal maneuverings taking place in federal courts. At the end of the three weeks, the army was finally summoned to escort us to school.

The military personnel were well-trained and highly efficient; and they were, mainly, all white. A command decision had been made to leave the black soldiers at the base rather than assign them to duties at Central. A few black soldiers were on the premises at Central, but not in plain view. It was felt that white southerners would object even more strenuously to this "occupation" if black soldiers were there.

Another very odd thing: None of the troops had ammunition for their weapons. I did not know this until years after the fact; but again, a command decision had been made on the assumption that a blood bath might erupt if the soldiers were forced to use their rifles. And it would have been very difficult to explain such a thing to the American people.

But even with the army there, we were terrorized on a daily basis. Whatever you can imagine one human being doing to another—that was probably done to us that year. We were beaten down both physically and psychologically by the time school was finally over for the year. And what always fascinated me was the ease with which these kids could do things to us. With a sense of impunity they kicked, shoved, slapped, tripped, spat upon, derided, sneered, belittled, and otherwise tried to make life miserable for us.

We had taken a vow of nonviolence that year, having been urged to do so by Martin Luther King, Jr., who had come to

Little Rock to meet with us. He, along with Jim Lawson and Glenn Smiley, spent time helping us to understand the essence of nonviolence. We decided that being nonviolent made sense, and agreed to do it. Our tormentors, however, were not people who could understand or appreciate the nuances of such a way of behaving. To them we were simply stationary targets, and they took full advantage of the situation.

I will never forget the look on the faces of the people who confronted us each day at school. I would replicate for you the twisted up countenances I observed that year, but frankly, I don't know how any human being manages to screw up his or her face in such a manner. And out of those faces would spew forth the vilest language you could imagine. They talked about us, our parents, especially our mothers. They seemed to think they were well-informed about the maternal side of our families; and they offered travel advice, free, non-solicited detailed information about where we should go and how we should get there. In retrospect, I can treat the whole thing with a bit of humor; but let me assure you, it was no laughing matter at the time.

There were far more serious encounters during that school year, and I had to call on all the resources at my command to get through those experiences. One day as I sat in the auditorium—on the back row, of course, so that I could easily escape any planned mayhem—I felt a hard kick. The chairs were made of a thin plywood, so I got the full thrust of the kicker's forward momentum. I turned to see who it was, and there was an angry white male student glaring at me. His nonverbal statement, according to my interpretation, was: "I don't like you and I want to hurt you!" I say this because it occurred to me at that point in time that if he had simply wanted to get my attention, he could have used a less aggressive approach.

On another occasion, as I walked down the hallway on the first floor of the school building, a passing student leaned toward me and let fly with a thick wad of spittle, which covered my entire face, and dripped down over my chest. I remember thinking, "I don't know what to do in this kind of circumstance." I knew that we had chosen nonviolence as our response option, but here was something that seemed to demand a different kind of response. My mind was muddled, and I was greatly afraid as well.

Here again was that fear that seemed never too far away on any of my days at Central. I chose to continue walking, and wiped away as much of the vile liquid as I could until I could get to the bathroom to finish the clean up.

My psychological distress was much more profound than even the fear I felt at the time. How do you explain to yourself the choice to walk away and do nothing to counter the acts of the brute who had violated my sense of humanity? What words do you use to ease the mental turmoil that refuses to subside?

Even today I am haunted by that episode; and I am reminded of a similar incident that happened to Jim Lawson, one of the people who helped Martin Luther King, Jr., learn about nonviolence. Jim was sitting in a South Carolina restaurant during the sit-in movement, and a big, beefy, redneck type came over and spat directly into Jim's face. With his glasses covered by the viscous, vile looking discharge, Jim asked his attacker if he could borrow his handkerchief! I must say, I was not at that point in Little Rock, nor have I reached that point yet; but I do lean in that direction.

A part of my ability to cope with all of that came from my parents' storehouse of wisdom, and their resolve to participate in the process of change. I applaud both my parents for their willingness to confront a system so vile it robbed all participants of basic dignity. They saw beyond the ordinary, and were ready to do whatever it took to bring order and sanity to a world crazed by its own insistence on following mythological concepts.

I have been back to Little Rock on several occasions. I was hired by the city school board in 1998 as a desegregation consultant, and worked in that capacity for four years. As a consequence of being in Little Rock for extended periods of time, I bumped into many of the students who had been classmates in 1957. Several of them now work for the school system in

Little Rock as teachers, administrators, counselors, librarians, etc. They all said, "It wasn't me. I didn't participate in beating you up." On one occasion, I was confronted by a woman who informed me that she had been a student at Central during the 1957 school year; and she was still mad at me because the nine of us created such disturbance that the prom had been cancelled. I truly felt badly about the fact that she had missed the prom, but I assured her that we had no hand in that at all!

I learned much during that year of turmoil that has helped me navigate the racial terrain of America. One of the more salient lessons was that I cannot color code the universe. Not every single white person in Little Rock was my enemy, not every single black person was my friend. I learned as well that there are some people who believe in the sanctity of racial separation, and nothing that is said or done will ever change that. And there was another lesson learned well before my experience at Central High, but underscored by my experience there. And that lesson is that "what other people think about you is none of your business."

I learned, too, that love is a much stronger force than evil. We had opted, as I pointed out, to be nonviolent in our responses to brutality during that school year. Dr. Martin Luther King, Jr., had come to Little Rock, accompanied by the same Jim Lawson mentioned above and Glenn Smiley, two men who were helping him understand more about nonviolence. The three of them explained the basic concepts and urged us to consider adopting this philosophy. Dr. King further said that, while he wanted us to be nonviolent, we should know that it would not work unless we could with honesty say that we loved our enemies. In the end, we agreed that this was possible.

And later, in the halls of Central, I saw love at work. As I would stand and receive blows from an attacker without making any move to retaliate or to protect myself, the attacker would soon find himself unable to throw another blow. In those instances, I am convinced it was the power of love in action that made the difference.

Perhaps the most important lesson to emerge from that experience is that this country has yet to find the will or commitment to confront racism at its core. Oh, we still play games and engage in rhetorical exchanges that substitute for meaningful, substantive dialogue; but we do not demonstrate a desire to alter the status quo in ways that have meaning for masses of people. The elite among us seem to enjoy playing giant games of let's you and him fight; and many at the lower ends of the socioeconomic ladder lack the sophistication to even know they are pawns in the game.

As I look ahead in my attempt to make reasonable predictions about what the future might hold for us, I am alternately dismayed and delighted. Dismayed because we seem to have lost our way, and our spiritual compass has not worked for years; delighted because at times I see the light of recognition in the eyes of young people who know that anything is possible if we want it to happen. They, the potential leaders of our wayward society, exhibit signs of willingness to cast off the mantle of greed-based consumerism, and look for new answers to the ongoing problems we face.

There are no easy answers to be found, that much is certain. But, when those who feel the impulse to engage in the search begin to prepare themselves for the task, we can expect miracles and wonders. Hyperbole, you say. Perhaps, but I do believe firmly in the resilience of the human spirit. Energy can be unleashed when we agree to rearrange our mental maps to exclude all lines of separation between people; when we treat each other as peers in the universe; when we see each other as we are without need to evaluate or judge; when we choose to bear witness to truth and justice.

A few months ago I attended a lecture by Jamaica Kincaid, who spoke passionately about a number of contemporary issues. She spoke about the evils of racism, and the harm caused by those who adhere to its principles. At the end there was a question-and-answer session and a young white man stood and asked, "What can I do to help?" She responded: "Young man, there is nothing you can do to help. You see, what I want is for none of this ever to have happened; there is nothing you can do about that." Her words were poignant, searing, and created for me a frame of reference that contains the seeds of positive change.

If all of us were to dedicate ourselves to doing those things that could lead to the development of a world unlike any we have seen thus far, perhaps Jamaica Kincaid and all those she spoke for could find ways to balance life's equations so that the past and present inequities would not loom so large. Yes, we need to know the historical antecedents, because they dictate present choices and inform systemic responses. Yet we need also to learn how to alter the course of human action, so that the mistakes of the past are not repeated in the present. And, we need high-level awareness about the present, so that we are not confused about how the influences of the past are manifested, so our alterations are not in vain.

As an example of what I am saying here, let me share with you this insight I gained in a federal courthouse in Little Rock. As I sat there awaiting my turn to testify in a school-related action, I was struck by the scene that unfolded around me as I glanced around the room. On the walls of that courthouse are framed portraits of all the past justices of the court. There they were in their monochromatic, male-gendered reality. I sat there in sort of a daze, because I realized in that instant that this was the same courthouse where young fourth graders would come for their lessons in American justice. Their eyes would take in that same scene, but there would be no mention of how and why this came to be. The current presiding judge would come forth attired in his robes and give them his version of the national narrative, but he would not address the reality of the faces on the wall. The fourth graders would leave the courthouse in a state of cognitive dissonance; their young minds would record the scene, but there would be no accompanying explanation. They would have to figure it out for themselves. If only they knew what it was they had to figure out!

I am a grandfather now. My two grandsons, PJ and Austin, live in Marietta, Georgia. I talk to them all the time about life in these United States. The information we consider represents my attempt to prepare them for the national narrative they will most surely encounter as they enter the formal institutions of education in this country.

I want them to think critically about the issues, to make healthy choices, to know that they must develop the skills required to successfully navigate the terrain if they are to survive. I would prefer not to have these conversations. I would enjoy more spending time with them exploring the beauty of the universe; moving freely about the world, taking in the sights and sounds, and developing together our creative potential. At ages four and one year, it is not always easy for me to know if they understand what I am saying to them; but I continue to speak my truth in their presence.

Finally, as we come to a close tonight, it is my hope that you will find ways to challenge the status quo. Go naked to the mirror and ask these questions: "By what action of mine was the status quo supported today? Am I willing to change what I do?"

My friend and colleague Eloise Klein Healy once wrote, "If what you know doesn't change you, change what you know." Go forth, and learn!

Caring Enough to Confront

Presentation to UCLA Black Faculty and Staff

Thursday, January 15, 1998

Problems and issues that combine to cause us mental grief and frustration are often left to fester and grow because we are not willing and/or able to confront the stark realities around us. Chaos has replaced community, and we are stuck in the midst of the madness without hope or reason to feel better about the future. Cover all of this with an overlay of endemic racism, and it is easy to see how some individuals, families, and societal groups engage primarily in behaviors designed to protect them from real and imagined danger. The salient task of building a viable community is postponed in the name of survival. But, ironically, true survival can come only as a product of a healthy, dynamic community.

In his efforts to help move us toward a state of true community, M. Scott Peck suggests a road that leads through chaos. His analysis of the way we interact includes a view that pseudo-community is our most prevalent state of being. To create community, this unreasonable facsimile must be destroyed; and it is this task that promises chaos, the precursor to a preferred way of life.

To some it may seem incongruous to plan a state of disruption as part of a quest for communal existence. Yet it is vital that non-functional systems be removed if our potential to live together in healthy ways is to be realized. Martin Luther King,

Jr., understood this concept well. He was not afraid to challenge accepted societal norms and behaviors. His vision was not clouded by a philosophy of human interaction that would value one group of people more than others. He cared enough to confront. And it is our opportunity, as we move into the 21st Century, to care enough to confront self and each other in the name of establishing and maintaining communities that support and sustain efforts to grow spiritually, socially, economically, mentally, physically, and psychologically.

A few years ago I picked up a copy of David Augsburger's book entitled *Caring Enough to Confront*, and was immediately convinced of the efficacy of his suggested approach to relationships. He shows how the two words, "caring" and "confronting," can be combined into a neologism he calls "carefronting." This new term unites the love of caring with the power of confronting.

We will not expend the copious amounts of energy necessary to confront effectively if we don't care about the others involved. But, when we do care, confronting looms as the most desirable option. A mother whose child has a penchant for playing too close to the curb of a busy street will not hesitate to confront her progeny; she will not stand idly by and risk the possibility of seeing her child swept under the wheels of a passing vehicle. The child, in the way of many children, may attempt to disobey the mother, and continue the death-defying activity on the edge of the roadway, at least initially. But love for her baby will compel the mother to take whatever measures are necessary to convince the errant toddler to remain safely in the yard. Carefronting communicates truth, love, and respect.

In his "Letter From Birmingham Jail," Martin Luther King, Jr., spoke truth in love to those who urged him to back off, to wait for a more propitious moment. He addresses the letter to: "My Dear Fellow Clergymen." In the body of the letter he reminds them of their recent statement calling his activities "unwise and untimely." He then follows with an explanation of why he is in Birmingham, and how nonviolent confrontation attempts to bring about positive changes. In nine pages of single-spaced copy, Dr. King seeks to inform and instruct his readers about the necessity for direct action, not passive observation hoping things will somehow magically change.

Note this excerpt from his letter:

> *Moreover, I am cognizant of the interrelatedness of all communities and states. I cannot sit idly by in Atlanta and not be concerned about what happens in Birmingham. Injustice anywhere is a threat to justice everywhere. We are caught in an inescapable network of mutuality, tied in a single garment of destiny. Whatever affects one directly, affects all indirectly. Never again can we afford to live with the narrow, provincial "outside agitator" idea. Anyone who lives inside the United States can never be considered an outsider anywhere within its bounds.*

In 1968, just prior to his assassination, Dr. King was planning to "dislocate" day-to-day life in America's major cities in an effort to force the United States government to alter its policies and practices vis-à-vis citizens of color "to compel unwilling authorities to yield to the mandates of justice." His support of massive civil disobedience frightened many of his followers, but others began to see the rationale for such a strategy.

Andrew Young, speaking about the Southern Christian Leadership Conference's position at that time, said: "We have accepted the challenge to so threaten nonviolently the self-interest of the powers that be that they will be able to change, that they will see that a change is necessary. Our threat will be so pointed and well-defined that they will know that a change is possible and will change in the right direction."

His optimism possibly was founded upon an understanding of human interaction that suggests: When you act in ways designed to deprive another of something valuable, that person will most likely agree to a compromise to avoid total loss. Not altogether a certain strategy, especially in a country with a long history of genocide, enslavement, internment, de jure and de facto segregation, and a willingness to embrace proponents of white supremacy at every level of government, business, education, and social interface.

But, I do think Martin Luther King, Jr., was indeed planning a Gandhi-like assault on the conscience of America, something that superseded marches, rallies, and regional boycotts. In Memphis, where he died, he was attempting to organize garbage collectors across racial and ethnic lines. It was clearer than ever to him that poverty respects no skin color; all people are vulnerable to this egregious condition.

In the face of the ongoing crisis in 1998, we are the vanguard. We hold the privilege, if you will, of deciding what to do. And it makes sense to think about weaving strands together to make strong communities. The process must include confrontation; the evils must be named and called out. In the 21st Century we must abandon the practices of looking the other way, wringing our hands in frustration, expecting problems to disappear like magic, and failing to use the knowledge and resources at hand.

And we start with self. Yes, the beginning steps take place within that 36-inch circumference describing what many in today's parlance refer to as one's personal space. You see, the primary building block for any community is self.

Question: "Do you care enough to confront self? Are you willing to ask the hard questions that can lead to eventual change if your commitment does not falter? If you are prepared to do so, you can become a positive force in all the communities where you have membership. If not, we are all in trouble, because no community is stronger than its weakest member. We depend upon each other to make healthy choices. To the extent that we do, the goal of creating viable communities is more fully realized.

Next, we must learn to be in relationship to each other such that the interaction is mutually beneficial, and that the outcomes of our connections continue to propel us forward toward the desired goals. It is here that caring enough to confront can be a center-stage reality, where this philosophy is put to the ultimate test.

Often we will not confront each other because of our reluctance to stir up emotions, or because of fears of being misunderstood, or any number of reasons that you and I know well. Yet, until we are willing to take the risk of being "real" in our relationships, the idea of community remains just that, an idea.

This same task is required at the next level, that of family group. Confronting those who constitute family can lead to a reshaping of social dynamics, and the development of structures that allow for the speedy resolution of problems and the consistent planning necessary to exist beyond levels of mere survival.

Continuing this line of thought, we wind up in a world community characterized by decisions made at each level reflecting principles of true community—obviously an ideal with no visible signs of support, unless, of course, we were willing to start today making individual decisions in harmony with this ideal.

Augsburger says, even though we know it already, confronting is hard work. But he goes on to say, life without confrontation is directionless, aimless, passive. When unchallenged, human beings tend to drift, to wander, or to stagnate. Confrontation is a necessary stimulation to jog one out of mediocrity or to prod one back from extremes. Confrontation is an art to be learned.

And what better arena to learn to confront self and others than racism in America? Many years ago on this campus, in the main auditorium in Royce Hall, I sat on the front row listening to Dr. Kenneth Clark give guidelines and directions for confronting racism. He spoke eloquently and passionately about things with which I was only too familiar. I was poised with pencil and pad, ready to jot down anything that might help me understand more completely what racism was about, and how I might deal with it more effectively in my own life.

Disappointingly, he ended his presentation with this statement: "I fear that white America will devise ways to live in the ocean before they will ever agree to social equality for black

Americans." He went on to say that often he was so discouraged that the thought of packing up his family and moving to Montego Bay seemed the most useful option.

My thought was that, if Kenneth Clark, a respected and admired psychologist, felt this way, what chance did I have to make sense of this racist society? Now, some 30-plus years later, I have a better grasp of what actually happened there in Royce Hall. Clark was being as honest as he could be about the reality of life in this country, but he was also committed to making positive changes. His despair was real, but not final.

In order for us to build a true community, we must not back away from the harsh reality around us. There are those, for instance, who cry aloud in support of what they deem an appropriate perspective for us: a colorblind society. These proponents want me to ignore obvious physical realities. They would have me voluntarily disable myself.

I say, in a true community we honor and embrace differences. We understand that difference is not negative; that it is merely descriptive. The judgments we make about difference have no place in a community of peers who respect uniqueness and individuality.

As we think about confronting racism, it is quickly apparent that we have absorbed much of the racist ideology that surrounds us. We are reluctant to confront, and the task is made more difficult by the fact that much of the confrontation process is visceral and not cerebral. There is gut-level involvement. There are allegiances to significant others in our life. Fear looms on the horizon. And we have to double check: Do I really care enough to confront?

I urge you today to make a personal commitment to confront self and others in the name of building strong communities. Communities that are not defined by the racial and ethnic labels so much a part of our lexicon, but ones that reflect a higher-level understanding about the potential of humanity to rise above the barriers imposed by our own unwillingness to think and dream beyond the ordinary.

I would like to end with the same words Martin Luther King, Jr., used to close his "Letter From Birmingham Jail":

> *Let us all hope that the dark clouds of racial prejudice will soon pass away and the deep fog of misunderstanding will be lifted from our fear-drenched communities, and in some not too distant tomorrow the radiant stars of love and brotherhood will shine over our great nation with all their scintillating beauty.*
>
> *Yours for the cause of peace and brotherhood,*
> *Martin Luther King, Jr.*

Choosing Nonviolence: The Courage to be Different

Talk presented at The Eighth Annual Ecumenical Black Campus Ministry Scholarship Luncheon at UC San Diego in Honor of Dr. Martin Luther King, Jr.

Thursday, January 16, 1992

As citizens of these United States of America we inherit a legacy of violence. As visitors to these shores you experience the fruits of this legacy in its myriad manifestations. Together we suffer the effects of centuries-old responses to life's conflicts.

Recently I accepted an invitation from my mom to address her genealogical society. They wanted to know about the availability of public records pertaining to the existence of African Americans in the State of Arkansas. This is not to suggest that I knew anything about such matters. But when your mom tells her fellow club members that her son, the Ph.D., will speak to the issue, he scurries around to gather information to present.

In doing so, I looked into the history of Arkansas to develop a frame of reference for my remarks. I found mountains of evidence to support the notion that I was born in a state with a long history of violence. In 1837, John Wilson, speaker of the first state House of Representatives, murdered Representative Joseph J. Anthony on the House floor. In response to criticism from Anthony, Wilson drew a Bowie knife and stabbed him to death in front of all assembled. A subsequent trial ended with a jury verdict of "excusable homicide."

This, I submit, is but one of the more blatant examples of violent behavior threaded throughout the fabric of this nation. It is not unlike the violence we read about in 1992 reports of our daily activity; nor is it different from the postures we assume in the face of those we would label our enemies. It was by labeling them our enemies that we were able to justify bombing the Iraqis into the 14th century.

During the Vietnam War, I wrote the following poem to grapple with the violence I saw around me:

WE, THE PEOPLE…

Ignorance, Incompetence, imbedded in the soul.
Like dye-stained fabric resisting the efforts
Of the master cleaner,
Dull-witted morons afloat in a sea of knowledge,
No absorption, no remembrance.

Destined to live to follow the leader
Who, like Thurber's owl
Leads us down the highway's center stripe
Headlong into the noonday traffic.

Where do we go from here?
Indeed, where the hell are we?
Black v. White
Left v. Right
Us v. Them

We the people… yes,
We the people do ordain and establish
This chaos, this madness, this perverse comedy,
This ludicrous facsimile of life.

The nightshade is drawn and no light is seen.
Groping and stumbling, unknowing, unable, unwilling
To stem the flow of bright red blood.
Accustomed to the crimson glow.

Curtail the bombing but do not stop.
There are many yet alive who aspire to be the enemy.
We must not encourage the enemy.
We must chastise, Christianize, democratize the enemy.

One nation, trying hard
To quicken the pace
And shorten the road
To hell.

And it has not been merely the physical destruction of our fellow human beings that constitutes the violence of our lives. We wreak havoc on each other with words and indirect action as well. Words designed to kill as surely as an AK47. Actions taken in secret or in the full light of day with the intent to defraud, misdirect, mislead, confuse, overwhelm, or mystify. We take pride even in our ability to master such tactics; and may, from time to time, be decorated with ribbons and medals for our efforts. We justify our actions by blaming the other for "starting it." If we can show with little doubt that someone else provoked the action, we can do anything we want to do with impunity; or so goes much of the conventional wisdom about human interaction.

From the time we are pushed on the nursery school playground and feel righteous about pushing back, to responding in kind to the underhanded schemes of a competitor in school or at work, we build continuously a foundation with a cornerstone of violent thought and action.

Indeed, it is not hard to develop a response system based on this seemingly universally accepted dictum of eye for an eye, tooth for a tooth. It has the ring of moral acceptability. There is social support for "You hit me. I'll hit you back."

In second grade my child was assaulted by a peer who gave no warning or reason for the attack. In response, my daughter sought the protection and wisdom of the teacher who said to her, "You hit her back!" This of course was contrary to all that she had learned from her parents. Her feeble efforts to comply with the teacher's directions resulted in further pain and greater confusion about her own choice of response. We had instructed both daughters to appeal to the adult authority in charge if and when such a situation should ever arise; but the adult in this case abdicated her responsibility, at least by my reckoning. But, as you consider your own pattern of growth and development, I would venture to guess that most of you would opt for the "self-protection" mode rather than rely on the efforts of an authority figure.

Have you ever listened closely to the violent words we use in communicating with each other? We call each other names and laugh together at the antics of Homey the Clown who verbally and physically abuses those around him. We create languages to convey our messages of hatred and exclusion.

The language of racism, sexism, and classism is but one illustration of this dynamic quality of our existence. What you say matters. The old axiom, "Sticks and stones may break my bones, but words can never hurt me," does not tell the whole truth. Some words spoken by some people can hurt more than the sticks and stones.

The real question is why do we engage in this form of interaction, since it does little to enhance the aggressor or the victim? Some years ago I chanced upon this statement by Ernest Becker in a work entitled *The Birth and Death of Meaning*: "It is the task of culture to provide each person with the conviction that he or she is an object of primary value in a world of meaningful action."

Culture has failed to provide that conviction for so many. As my wife and I walked along White Cottage Road in the northern end of the Napa Valley where we lived for ten years, a car occupied by two young Anglo males drove by, and as they passed us, the passenger leaned out of the window and yelled as loudly as he could, "NIGGERS!" A violent intrusion; an unnecessary shattering of a peaceful ambience; a violation of the cultural dictate.

The America into which Martin Luther King, Jr., was born in 1929 offered him the same legacy of violence we see erupting around us in 1992. His response was courageous: he opted for nonviolence. He chose to turn left in the face of so many hundreds of thousands who turned right. He went against the grain because he believed that we could align ourselves with higher moral forces and defeat those who would use violence and aggression. His goal was harmony among all groups of people living in this country, and the ability of all to come together to solve problems of mutual concern. He challenged a supporting pillar of our social existence—that each citizen has the right to use violence in certain lawfully defined situations.

The question we confront today, underscored by the theme of this gathering, is this: *Can* we save ourselves, *can* we save our children from the violence that threatens to decimate an entire generation of African-American males? The answer lies dormant within each one of us to some degree, in that it depends upon the choices we are willing to make, and the energy we are willing to invest in creating a nonviolent approach to life.

As a child growing up in the American South, I was eyewitness to violence of every sort. Violence within groups, between groups, among families, among friends as well as enemies, in highly respected social circles, in the streets of Little Rock, in the conversations of people everywhere. I recall vividly the news reports informing us about the murder of Emmett Till. It was especially frightening to me, since I was the same age as Emmett, and what was to stop those same forces of violence from crossing the border between Mississippi and Arkansas? Or even, from igniting such forces already resident in my hometown?

A few years after this episode I was presented with the opportunity to participate in the desegregation of Little Rock's Central High School. In the spring of 1957 I responded "yes" to the query, "Would you be interested in attending Central High

School in the fall?" Eventually there were nine of us who actually did integrate the school.

As part of the preparation for that task, Martin Luther King, Jr., came to Little Rock and offered counsel about using nonviolence as a response to the opposition we would undoubtedly face. Jim Lawson and Glenn Smiley, two of King's nonviolence teachers, instructed us in the finer points of this philosophy. We did adopt nonviolence as our mode of response, and were afforded ample opportunity to practice this method once we entered the school. I won't recite here the litany of insults, the hateful actions, or the failures of authority figures to act responsibly toward us; but suffice it to say, we were not welcome in that environment!

Well before the Central High experience, however, I was convinced that violence was a poor choice for anybody. The young males in my peer group often fought each other to demonstrate physical superiority, or to defend perceived attacks on their manhood or the virtue of family members, particularly mothers.

It was never my inclination to adopt this behavior as my own. I chose to respond differently, based on my notion that we could exist at higher levels; that we could engage in problem solving without mutual destruction. I think these ideas came as a direct result of teachings from the church, combined with input from adults who were interested in my well-being and survival.

Young African-American males today are faced with situations that call for creative responses. We all know that if the continued response to life in these United States is violence, the losers will be those who feel they have no stake in the future of this country. With nothing to lose anyway, life becomes cheap and expendable. The police forces of the nation agree, and all guns are pointed at those who bear the stamp of social outcast, social anomaly, social pariah. This combination of self-destroying behavior and officially sanctioned homicide is perhaps our most disturbing picture of violence in this country today.

The answers are not readily apparent as we delve into the information at our disposal. As we have seen, the history of violence serves as a backdrop for today's responses to the stresses of life. Those who would promote a different approach, as did Dr. King, often fall victim to those same forces of violence they seek to diminish. It is possible, however, to make a personal commitment to abhor violence in your own life. To choose actions and responses that demonstrate a growing awareness of the need for a way of life that enhances, rather than destroys, the human organism.

A nonviolent approach to life does not mean that you offer your body in sacrifice for a cause, but that you develop an awareness of how your choice of response can support or diminish the potential for violence. If someone says something or does something that seems contrary to what you expected or wanted, don't use that as an opportunity to "give him a piece of your mind." Commit yourself to reasonable and rational problem solving.

Be willing to work hard to elect to office those people who will state clearly their intention to promote systems of government that lead to harmonious interaction between all people. Don't be afraid to question any politician whose stance is suspect on issues of importance. If enough sensitive people would choose to become politically active, we could avoid some of the unbearable situations we now face at local and national levels.

Discover ways in which you can effectively counteract the messages that support violence currently available to our children. Movies, television programs, music videos, and other forms of entertainment use themes of violence because the financial rewards for the performers and producers of these violent episodes are so great that they churn out even more in the name of even higher profits. But what if we did not buy their products? You can confront your own children with information about the danger of such messages, and also provide alternative ways for them to be entertained.

I recall researching information on the impact of rock music when my own daughters were very young. I was able to find data on the anapestic rock beat which is antithetical to the natural heartbeat. I went with them to a rock concert to give them the benefit of my on-the-spot observations about the potential damage to the body when it is exposed overmuch to rock's anapestic beat. They were not thrilled, to put it mildly. But it was done with the intent of helping them to develop more discerning attitudes and sensibilities about the world around them.

Teach younger people around you, based on your own experience, how habits that support mutual sharing and mutual aid can lead to attitudes of harmony and peace. Demonstrate in your own life how easy it is to choose actions that promote growth and positive development.

Read as much and as often as humanly possible. I counsel students to read at least one book per week on topics of interest and concern to them. I say the same to you. Information is available in libraries throughout this country. It's available in bookstores, living rooms, basements, attics, wherever books are stored. Become acquainted with that information and use it in creative ways.

Initiate activities in your own neighborhood designed to help focus attention on matters of import. In the Pasadena/Altadena area, we have developed the African American Cultural Institute which will begin its Saturday School program on February 1, 1992. The goal is to provide opportunity for African Americans to learn ways of improving their own circumstances by building a storehouse of knowledge and information about a variety of subjects, including history and historical dimensions. Emphasis on basic skill development will be an integral part of the program as well.

It is no easy assignment to reverse ways of responding that have become habitual. It is important to realize, however, that such a task is manageable. Be willing to commit your time and energy in the name of learning, and teaching others how to learn—to go forth and create a world eager to embrace nonviolence as the only viable way to live.

Creating the Beloved Community

Talk presented at the NCCJ 13th Annual
Dr. Martin Luther King, Jr., All People's Breakfast
Long Beach, California

Monday, January 15, 2001

"Creating the beloved community." The resonance of the phrase and the imagery it calls forth is a catalyst that triggers a chain reaction of memories and mind-pleasing associations for me. The kaleidoscope of images, the voices of admonition and exhortation, the easy laughter, the smiles, the hugs, the blessed assurance of being part of a group of people who loved me without reservation—all these come flooding in to remind me of the value and the absolute necessity of living in true community. It is here, in the midst of those who give their love in abundance, that individuals prosper and grow; rise to meet the challenges of life with confidence and the expectation of success; strive mightily to maximize whatever potential may be theirs; rest peacefully at day's end, knowing that prayers are being raised on their behalf, and, finally, dream the sweet dreams of souls content to be integral parts of a loving, embracing, protecting, sustaining, and forgiving community.

This was life for me in Little Rock, Arkansas, in the middle of the 20th Century. The beloved community was imagined, and displayed in myriad forms throughout my early life in

Little Rock. It was my privilege to have a glimpse, to taste and see how good it can be to have the nurture and support of a community of people solidly in my corner. It was all the more poignant because it became clear to me all too quickly that outside the narrow confines of the black community, I was not beloved at all.

No, the concept of community was altered drastically and convincingly as I ventured out into the wider arena of life. The messages were unmistakable—in words written and spoken, in law and social custom, from academic podiums and pastoral pulpits, in the fractured English favored by backwater bigots, in the cultivated language of political opportunists, from everywhere it seemed came the loud, raucous cry, "Terry Roberts, you don't count for much in this world."

It was hard to navigate the terrain of a city plastered with signs reading "Men," "Women, "Colored." It was not easy to make that long trek to the back of the bus, fully aware that even the rear seat was not promised. I am reminded of a scene from one of the "Eyes on the Prize" series. A southern sheriff addresses Charles Sherrod, a black civil rights worker: "Sherrod, it's just mind over matter: I don't mind, and you don't matter."

Martin Luther King, Jr., understood the need to build a true community: one that was not crisscrossed by lines of demarcation, not a Balkanized collection of color-coded enclaves, but a society of human beings working together to accomplish shared goals and objectives. The beloved community includes everybody. There are no outsiders.

In his "Letter From Birmingham Jail," Dr. King speaks assertively to his fellow clergymen who had publicly chided him for coming to Birmingham to stir up trouble. He makes a special point of explaining how, in true community, there can be no such person as an outside agitator. After decrying the fact that the opposing clergy seem to have been influenced by the view which argues against outsiders coming in, Dr. King reveals his insider identity.

He does it first by carefully delineating his organizational ties with the Southern Christian Leadership Conference (SCLC). It was the SCLC that invited him to Birmingham to lead peaceful demonstrations against the egregious segregationist policies and practices that kept the community divided by lines drawn in color. And then Dr. King writes: "But more basically, I am in Birmingham because injustice is here. Like Paul, I must constantly respond to the Macedonian call for aid." You see, if we truly want to live in community, we have to accept that the idea of community is larger than our imagination; it exists beyond our capacity to comprehend, and will guide us toward a more enlightened existence if we allow the concept to expand in our minds.

The following words spoken by Dr. King bring us even closer to an understanding of the beloved community: "An individual has not started living until he can rise above the narrow confines of his individualistic concerns to the broader concerns of humanity." (CSK, 1983) All of us have to be willing to move beyond self if we want to find the parameters of the beloved community. Dr. King and his colleagues knew this well in 1957 when they formed the Southern Christian Leadership Conference. They chose as their motto: "To Save the Soul of America." (Trumpet, 1967) It was not about saving my soul, or our souls, but the soul of the entire nation. And I am convinced, given the pathways he sought, based on the directions in which he was leaning, the tenor and tone of his public orations, that had he lived longer, Dr. King's vision of a beloved community extending beyond these national shores would have been more than evident.

Listen to his voice as he muses about the future: "Our hope for creative living in this world house that we have inherited lies in our ability to reestablish the moral ends of our lives in personal character and social justice. Without this spiritual and moral reawakening we shall destroy ourselves in the misuse of our own instruments." (CSK, 1983)

But before we tackle the "world house," we need to sweep clean the floor where we live. By far, the most persistent, confusing, and confounding barrier to building true community in this nation is the mythological construct of race.

As Cornel West so aptly put it, "Race matters." It matters personally, socially, politically, spiritually, locally, nationally, consistently, and perpetually. It shapes our thinking about who we are and who others may or may not be. It interferes with our ability to focus on merit or character, and clouds our mental maps with the ideological vapors of racism and the dense fog of white supremacy. Not only does race matter, it causes pain and agony for individuals who find themselves on the bottom rung of the racial hierarchy, for families where favors are granted to members whose skin tone approximates the racial ideal, for communities where lines of separation by race become battle zones, for all people who find it impossible to escape the racialized reality that defines all social, legal, political, and business transactions in their world.

"Ever since the birth of our nation, white America has had a schizophrenic personality on the question of race. She has been torn between selves—a self in which she proudly professed the great principles of democracy and a self in which she sadly practiced the antithesis of democracy… The majority of white Americans consider themselves sincerely committed to justice for the Negro. They believe that American society is essentially hospitable to fair play and to steady growth toward a middle-class Utopia embodying racial harmony. But unfortunately this is a fantasy of self-deception and comfortable vanity… Laws are passed in a crisis mood after a Birmingham or a Selma, but no substantial fervor survives the formal signing of legislation. The recording of the law in itself is treated as the reality of the reform." (Chaos, 1967)

Dr. King's understanding of racism took him beyond the ordinary limits of discourse about the possibilities for change in our society. He was not afraid to give voice to the reality as he saw it in the name of seeking a viable alternative.

"The roots of racism are very deep in America. Historically it was so acceptable in the national life that today it still only lightly burdens the conscience... For the good of America, it is necessary to refute the idea that the dominant ideology in our country even today is freedom and equality while racism is just an occasional departure from the norm on the part of a few bigoted extremists."

"To live with the pretense that racism is a doctrine of a very few is to disarm us in fighting it frontally as scientifically unsound, morally repugnant, and socially destructive. The prescription for the cure rests with the accurate diagnoses of the disease. A people who began a national life inspired by a vision of brotherhood can redeem itself. But redemption can come only through a humble acknowledgment of guilt and an honest knowledge of self." (Chaos, 1967)

It is necessary also to get rid of that false notion that there is some miraculous quality in the flow of time that inevitably heals all evils. (Chaos, 1967) Time itself is neutral. Choices made in time and space dictate the range of options to follow any given set of choices, but this requires action in time, not time alone.

In that same "Letter From Birmingham Jail," Dr. King explains the irrational nature of thinking that time will serve to end all racist practices. He proposes that the clergy seek to actualize those principles that speak to the reality that deeply rooted in our religious heritage is the conviction that every man is an heir to a legacy of dignity and worth. (Chaos, 1967) And to that I would add that whatever is done must be calculated to achieve the goal of true community. "A vigorous enforcement of civil rights laws will bring an end to segregated public facilities, but it cannot bring an end to fears, prejudice, pride, and irrationality, which are the barriers to a truly integrated society." (Chaos, 1967)

In fact, to create a community that meets this standard, we have to accept a process that frightens some and seems unwise to others. Scott Peck speaks to this issue in his writings about finding true community. His notion is that we must first endure the chaos of dismantling the pseudo-community in which we now live; that we have to live with the rawness exposed when we peel away the thin veneer of civility that characterizes our interactions. It is only when we are willing to take on this task that we can expect to encroach upon the boundaries of true community. It will not be a matter of ease and comfort.

More than anything else, I can promise you pain and discomfort along the pathway to the beloved community. But know this as well: "The ultimate measure of a man is not where he stands in moments of comfort and convenience, but where he stands at times of challenge and controversy. The true neighbor will risk his position, his prestige, and even his life for the welfare of others. In dangerous valleys and hazardous pathways, he will lift some bruised and beaten brother to a higher and more noble life." (CSK, 1983)

And so, as you leave this place with a renewed vision of the beloved community, with an opportunity to participate fully and completely in its development, I exhort, urge, beg you to commit the life force that is yours to the realization of this dream shared with us in word and deed by Martin Luther King, Jr. The beloved community will remain forever a figment of our imagination unless we are willing to engage in the hard work necessary to bring it to fruition. I stand here today pledging my allegiance to the dream. I invite you to do the same. Together we will awaken the masses and march forward to the realms of true freedom and equality.

Reshaping the Mental Map: Cross-Cultural Life in the 21st Century

Talk presented at the Department of Veterans Affairs
Sepulveda, California

January 27, 1993

It is our ability to make sense out of the surrounding terrain that allows us to communicate and interact without total confusion and chaos. If this is acceptable wisdom, then how do we explain the harsh reality of continuous social explosion that suggests we have little ability to rightly interpret that which constitutes our environment? Perhaps it is because our mental maps have become outdated; useless artifacts that lead us into cul-de-sacs of despair and hopelessness, and which will insure finally that we remain disconnected and disillusioned even though we exist in a time and place bursting with potential for positive growth and fruitful expansion.

We start this journey ill prepared, and are forced to rely upon the guiding signals offered by significant others. Whether these others are benign or malignant forces is not something over which we have control. Indeed, it is my contention that one of the primary tasks of maturation is to review the inherited mental map provided by that person or those persons who occupy positions of power and authority in our lives.

After thorough review, the task can become one of change, alteration and restructuring, or one of underscoring and adding to what seems to be a tool worth keeping. In the main, it is the former that we must choose if positive growth is to be experienced. This reality is occasioned by the fact that very few of us escape the contamination of having been immersed in a social backwater—at times erroneously referred to as the main-stream—saturated with racism and its near relatives.

The mental map we start with forces us to define culturally different others in ways not conducive to mutually satisfying interactions. This is not to say that the rare individual does not transcend the ordinary to reach a point where he or she operates with a mental map that, when used appropriately, promotes equality of opportunity for all others and embraces a model of acceptance of all others as well, no matter how "different" they may appear to be. But, *rare* is the operative word in that sentence. The majority of us plod along blindly informed by social diagrams that do not display connections to all others. Indeed, some very significant lines are missing.

But, it is this process of connecting and the resulting relationships that help to create the foundations for a solidly based society; bases upon which we can build systems, institutions, agencies, collectives, and familial groups that reflect a growing understanding of the real possibilities inherent in our world. To begin this trek we do need new mental maps: creative guides to help us chart a course through the increasingly uncertain and uneven territory of these United States.

As we enter the 21st Century it is well to remember that we carry much excess baggage; and it would be prudent in the name of progress to dump some of this stuff before it contaminates another generation, even before one more decade has passed. You see, relationships are the vehicles by which and through which we communicate to each other. If we are not able to form viable relationships with those who are unlike ourselves, we run the risk of not being able to function at optimal levels.

If your mental map has not been updated, you are likely to approach a cross-cultural encounter with some caution or even trepidation. In fact, some maps instruct us to avoid certain people altogether. The information about the group to be excluded or shunned may contain descriptions of personality, behavior, customs, language, values, or beliefs to which we have assigned pejorative labels. The resultant negative images flood our minds, and make it impossible for us to view a member of the group in question with objectivity or empathetic understanding.

A professor of sociology told this story about himself: "During the time when I was a professor at the University of Arkansas at Fayetteville, I remember shopping at a local supermarket. The young woman at the cash register was an African American, and I found myself idly wondering if she would be able to compute correctly the amount to be charged, and whether she would give me the right change. Later, I realized that this way of thinking was an indication that I was picking up the attitudes and thought patterns of those around me, and I decided to seek a faculty position in California."

Perhaps the professor concluded that his mental map would be permanently solidified if he did not get out of the environment where negative images of African Americans abounded. It was no doubt an important transition for him; but I would add that the process of changing our mental map must go on in spite of the atmosphere around us. We live, work, and play in a racist, culturally insensitive society; and if positive change is to occur, it will have to happen in the midst of this onerous reality.

Let's take a look at one concept that is probably highly visible on the mental maps of all us assembled here. That concept is the one we call race. For thousands of years people were described as members of particular families, clans, tribes, as members of cities and states, as belonging to groups distinguished by their dress, language, and customs. It was only in the 19th Century that race was used as a category to describe people, and arguments mounted to support the notion that differences between people are based on racial characteristics.

In the realm of biology there is no such thing as race. Race is purely and simply a function of political and economic manipulation. In an article entitled "Ideology and Race in American History," historian Barbara J. Fields states: "The view that race is a biological fact, a physical attribute of individuals is no longer tenable. Race is a product of history, not of nature."

For most of us race is a convenient way to differentiate between people when the people in question closely resemble the racial definition we employ. This notion falls apart when we encounter someone who does not fit any given racial category. In spite of the growing difficulty of maintaining specific racial boundaries, we persist in holding on to what can best be described as an outmoded concept. But, such is the way of the mental map.

Consider the well-known anomaly of American racial convention that considers a white female capable of giving birth to a black child, but denies that a black female can give birth to a white child. It is clear to me that wholesale reshaping of American mental maps is in order. From a psychological viewpoint, it is obvious that mental health improves to the degree to which one is able to incorporate viable concepts and invigorating ideologies.

Using myself as an example, I will give you an idea of how this process of development and change comes to be. Development of and eventual change in the properties of the mental map, that is. Like you, I tumbled out of the womb at the appointed time and, while not quite a tabular rasa, I was rather sponge-like in my approach to life. Soaking up all that I found around me, I was no doubt convinced that my way of life was superior to all others, and that the people in my immediate social circle were to be emulated.

It took a few years for me to figure out that I could decide how to think and behave; I did not have to wait for instructions from others. To be sure, there are certain social risks involved here, not the least of which in some cases is the threat of disinheritance. Not a factor for me, of course, but still, it was somewhat disconcerting at times to know that my way of thinking no longer paralleled that of my parents in many respects.

In spite of the pain associated with growing into one's own, I was increasingly aware of the pleasure that comes with "finding things out!"

In time I confronted the images of race that had been instilled by well-meaning others in charge of my development. A burgeoning body of knowledge, fueled by what can only be described as an insatiable appetite for the written word, helped me to see the faulty cornerstones upon which this idea was based. It made no sense.

As a teenager, I became part of the group now known as the "Little Rock Nine," and continued my learning about things racial at Central High School in Little Rock, Arkansas. The reception provided for us by the white students at Central suggested that, in the main, they were not engaged in anything like the process I was experiencing. There seemed to be an acceptance of ideas and behaviors that relegated all people who were non-black into one camp and the remainder into some other place. Again, it made no sense.

Eventually I was able to design a map that helped me find a pathway through the cluttered terrain. Any idea that reduced human beings to categories was discarded. Thought patterns based on concepts of individual and group superiority or inferiority were reshaped to yield new patterns of peer relationships.

In a very exciting book entitled *Women's Reality*, Anne Wilson Schaef writes about the need to establish peer relationships with everybody else. She holds to the notion that only when we can relate as peers can we, together, rise above the dehumanizing "isms" that so confound us.

Additionally, it was my decision to confront actively any old ideas that emerged over time that were and are contrary to my new way of thinking and believing. I have embraced the concept that I am a citizen of the universe, and as such, I have a responsibility to broadcast the good news that you, too, qualify for that same label. Together, as we operate in the world as "good" citizens of the universe, we have the opportunity to create a space that has room for all. No one need be discarded!

Relationships across Lines of Demarcation

Presentation to San Bernardino City Unified School District

August 18, 2000

In his discussion of how true community is built, the author Scott Peck speaks about the need to foster chaos as a way of dismantling the veneer of pseudo-community in which most of us live. His thesis is simply this, if we care enough about living in true community with each other, we will risk going through chaos to make it happen.

The truth is, we don't have to manufacture chaos, it is upon us each and every day. So far, however, we have not figured out how to use the chaos as a springboard to something more substantive. Most of our energy goes into reacting to the events of the day; we don't have much left to put into creative thinking about how to develop viable, healthy communities.

And yet, your school district is very much involved in preparing community members to engage in the kind of work necessary to achieve the goal of true community. The supporters of true community in my Little Rock neighborhood offered a steady chorus of "Boy, get your education!" Following their advice contributed greatly to my determination to secure a formal education. I obtained a bachelor's degree in sociology; I earned an MSW at UCLA, and finished my formal work at Southern Illinois University in Carbondale, Illinois, where I was awarded a Ph.D. in psychology.

I have often dreamed about a society of individuals dedicated to learning, who will participate in relationships devoted to mutual growth and development; who will form communities of like-minded others; who will work toward building strong nations; who will actively seek to create a world based on cooperation and team effort with a goal of minimizing—dare I say eliminating—all urges toward destruction, selfishness and greed. A bit lofty perhaps, but worth a daydream or two.

One of the barriers to true community is our tendency to judge difference harshly. Coping positively with difference is not something that seems to arise naturally among populations of people. If anything, the reverse is true. The stage is set then for the school district to help students and community members learn how to deal with difference in ways that are healthy and productive.

In California, difference abounds. I would venture to say that every single person present here today can list ad hoc the various and sundry differences in race, culture, ethnicity, language, country of origin, and other such identifying characteristics that define your student population. It is within this mix that we find the seeds of change that can help the participants learn to honor and embrace difference, rather than vilify or judge harshly when a difference is perceived.

The schools are an ideal resource for helping community members confront issues about difference. Typically neighbors who are different, as measured by one dimension or another, will be classmates; they can learn directly how to communicate with each other. Programs especially designed for particular communities can be mounted on the campus of the local schools. Programs that fill the continuum from informational to experiential to academic to scholastic can reach a wide variety of community members. As students with similar goals and educational needs interact with each other, the opportunity to teach them how to cope with difference is apparent. There are other institutions in the community—i.e. the church, civic organizations, service clubs, etc.—but the school has an advantage in that most of the students are, by definition, open to learning. There are, of course, exceptions, but the majority of students are seeking a well-rounded education which could very well include instruction on how to cope positively with difference.

In the area of helping people learn about difference, it would be appropriate to consider the church as a prime institution, given the foundational principles and mission statements put forth by those bodies. Yet, we find repeatedly that many churches cater to monolithic congregations; the day of worship becomes even more segregated than ordinary days of the week.

The school has a distinct advantage in that all people are welcome all the time. The sheer proximity of different others provides opportunity for learning and growth. And when carefully considered programs and initiatives are launched, those opportunities are transformed into highly successful ventures along the road to an inclusive society.

Building competence and ability is yet another way in which schools can promote true community. Individuals who feel able to cope with life's demands, who are armed with skills and abilities, are much better equipped to participate fully in the dynamic of community life. By offering a variety of programs and classes to community members, the school becomes an invaluable resource for those who wish to increase skill and ability levels.

One of my favorite quotes comes from *The Birth and Death of Meaning*, a book written by cultural anthropologist Ernest Becker. In that work he writes: "It is the task of culture to provide each and every single individual with the firm conviction that he or she is an object of primary value in a world of meaningful action."

By helping students to develop competencies, by inviting community members to explore realms of knowledge, by assisting a host of learners to find their way in this world, you engage fully in the task Becker so eloquently describes. Also, you help assuage the hunger for ways to fill time and space. Human beings are ever in search of a viable agenda, a way to prove to self and others that there is meaning in life.

Let us look now specifically at the issues of hate and intolerance as they are manifested in our society. The proliferation of hate-mongering, especially through the use of the Internet, has reached crisis proportions. The most vulnerable in our society have to contend with concerted efforts designed to recruit them into the ranks of groups whose mission is to destroy hated others. These efforts to exclude have to be met by comparable efforts to include.

The role of the school district looms large in this regard since those who are most vulnerable are, generally speaking, those who are not well-educated. The task is not an easy one, nor will it be accomplished in a short span of time. Effective restructuring of mental maps to erase lines of demarcation that separate people from each other will not happen overnight.

This work demands what I call a fifth-level commitment, an agreement to do whatever it takes to accomplish the goal. The example set by the Yosemite Community College District in Modesto, California, is instructive. They have made a fifth-level commitment, and have dedicated resources and people power to developing curriculum for the coming school year. Chancellor Pam Fisher has decreed that all classes in all subjects must include information about issues of diversity in our population.

Suffice it to say, there is much more work to be done in this area than you may think. The good news is that it can be done, and it can be done with results that have lasting impact in any given community. The challenge is ours. The essential question: Are we willing to accept the responsibility? I urge you to commit at the fifth-level and go forth, secure in the knowledge that yours is a righteous cause.

Self: The Most Important Tool in Multicultural Intervention

Talk presented at the Biennial Conference of the Multicultural Research and Training Lab Pepperdine University, West Los Angeles Campus

Saturday, October 11, 2008

We make sense of the world and all that is in it based on data stored in our various mental compartments. The data collection process begins immediately upon our arrival in the universe. Fresh from a state of blissful preoccupation with the nuances of life as it is lived suspended in the amniotic bubble, we exit the womb and encounter a series of jarring sights, sounds, and physical intrusions. Even for those genetically endowed with fairly balanced temperaments, it is not the most propitious way to begin human existence. Initially we depend, totally and entirely, upon the goodness of others to supply basic necessities. In some cases this arrangement works to our advantage: We land in the laps of those who want nothing more than to insure our well-being. And, of course, at the other end of this spectrum we find those who would like nothing better than to rid themselves of the squalling, demanding creature that has suddenly, inexplicably landed in their midst.

Years ago I read Lisa Richette's disturbing book, *The Throwaway Children*, and realized how at-risk we all are simply as a consequence of having to rely on others to guarantee the wherewithal for our growth and development.

At some point along the continuum implied by my characterization, we locate ourselves. We find the space where we began, and remember the human beings assigned as our caretakers. Our look back in time brings a flood of complex emotions. For those assembled near the most positive edge, there are smiles, joyful memories, mind pictures that sparkle, remembered words of affirmation and genuine concern for overall well-being. But, as we approach the opposite end, lips begin to tremble, eyes moisten with tears, sphincters tighten, and clouds of gloom threaten to descend upon us.

Anything and everything you can imagine is represented along that bar, from love so deep it is hard to fathom to hatred so vile it defies any attempt to understand it. And yet, we survive; from whatever point of origin, some of us make it through the gauntlet thrown down by life, and find ways to prosper socially, culturally, financially, and spiritually. We develop strategies that allow us to confront life head-on, to play the hand dealt to us with skill and ability. And it is out of this crowd that we find clinicians who are uniquely qualified to intervene in the lives of fellow humans who have not yet solved some of life's basic problems.

Would that it were such a simple linear process! It is not. In truth, self is the most basic tool of intervention; but it is a tool in constant need of realignment, recalibration, reinvention, and recreation. An ever-evolving organism, self is vulnerable to myriad forces not all of which can be defined as synchronous with healthy growth. There are elements abroad that seek to destroy the foundations supporting healthy self-growth. This reality suggests, strongly, a need for self-awareness. A need to know the difference between the competing factors, and a level of commitment to choosing those things than enhance the self.

In my web browsing to discover the essence of the Multicultural Research and Training Lab (MRTL), I chanced upon a list that included the concepts of "critical mass and commitment." This set off a series of neural explosions revealing a now-opened memory bank; and I could see and hear Doug Glasgow in the late '60s at the UCLA School of Social Welfare imploring us to consider well the ramifications of commitment and critical mass. It was his observation that a critical mass of human beings could forever change the world, if they were so committed. I think he was right. If we would combine our energies, our collective life force, we could do great things, and do them very quickly!

But, I run ahead of my own agenda. First, we must understand how self gets to the point of even thinking beyond self! You are, to a person, already familiar with the ways in which psychologists have outlined the growth stages; from Freud to Maslow to Erikson and beyond, you have built your own mental models. The knowledge base you have created has served to help you understand and decipher much of what you see going on around you. My question to you today: Have you learned enough about yourself?

Specifically, since our focus is multicultural existence, have you learned about you as a multicultural person in this multicultural environment? In order to learn what is needful in this arena you must be willing to confront self at basic levels. The questions have to be posed in such a way as to elicit useful responses. There can be no glossing over the issues or avoiding the more difficult areas.

A few years ago, I appeared on a radio program sponsored by the local PBS outlet in Pasadena. A listener called in and invited me to lunch because he wanted to talk more in depth about the ideas I had presented about things racial in our community. We met for lunch a short time later, and he explained that he and several other of his colleagues had decided to meet monthly to confront each other about elements of racism each detected in the other. Their shared goal was to eliminate all vestiges of such thinking from their lives. He invited me to attend their next monthly session, and I saw them in action as they actively challenged each other to erase racist images and thoughts from their mental maps.

They demonstrated the efficacy of confrontation. Perhaps even more significant, they cared enough to confront. In his book by that title, *Caring Enough to Confront,* David Augsburger describes the ways in which we can reach higher levels of existence and the ways in which we can impel others toward those same heights. Augsburger combines the two notions of caring and confronting, and comes up with a new term: "carefronting." It is his thought that caring enough will lead us to confront others when they are imperiled by things that we can see but are invisible to the endangered persons.

Using this train of thought, I encourage each one of you to choose to carefront self; to go naked to the mirror and ask some of the hard questions that will lead you to new levels of understanding about who you are, especially in relationship to those around you who are different.

During my tenure at Antioch University, I was one of the faculty members who helped to create and teach a mandatory course entitled Society and the Individual. The course was designed to allow students opportunity to learn more about self, and to discover what actually happened at the intersection of self and other. The course was mandatory because most students would opt out of such a class, given the chance. As it was, they came kicking and screaming; but, at the end of the 10-week quarter, a majority could speak about the positive aspects of such a venture. Emotionally it was draining for all of us, teachers and students alike; but the results were well worth the effort.

You may bump into some forms of resistance as you take on this task of knowing self at more intimate levels. But I can assure you that, like the students at Antioch, you will find merit in the process. Out of this endeavor will come an even greater appreciation for the fact that you cannot use self as a barometer for the choice patterns, ideation, and political, social or cultural realities adopted by others. In some cases self-referent behavior is so habitual that it may be difficult to bring the other persons into focus; but stay with the process. After all, we are unique in the universe. No one of us is like any other one of us. One true benefit of carefronting self, and getting to know more about what happens at the intersection of self and others, is to learn about difference.

Difference is the one thing we all have in common. I know, there are many who suggest that if we focus on difference we will not see the similarities that ostensibly bind us together. I say, not so. We must understand difference first; we must learn to appreciate and embrace difference before even thinking about similarities.

In our investigation of difference, for instance, we learn about the concept of unequal oppression. A few centuries ago, James McCune Smith wrote about the concept of unequal oppression in relation to black people in this country. Extrapolating from his study of the matter, we can conclude that all of us are indeed unequally oppressed. We cannot afford to make judgments based on some idea of monolithic groups in society; there are no such entities. Within any given group of people, no matter how many may be the perceived ties that bind them together, there are some who are more or less oppressed than others in that same coterie. This is always true. Our task is to discover the story told by each individual, and to learn from that story, in part, who that person happens to be. And after we learn about this unique being in our presence, we can begin to figure out how to be in a meaningful, healthy, and growth-producing relationship with him or her.

You should know before I go along this road much farther, I am biased toward relationships. It is my thought that we are so constructed as human beings that we require meaningful relationships to survive. And further, I am biased toward what I have come to call the "collective," the entire array of people who inhabit this globe. As far as possible in my limited, prone-to-error existence, I strive to treat all others as my peers in this world. Whether I am able to do this in absolute terms is a question I must answer daily; but I am aware that I lean in this direction. My internal GPS system is attuned to the vital presence of others in the universe; and I chart my course to avoid undue collisions, and seek to cooperate with others to build a society that has room for all to thrive.

In many ways I feel fortunate to have learned some critical life lessons early in the game. My mom taught me at age seven or so that race was a bogus construct, that it had absolutely no scientific validity. It was an idea introduced to the lexicon by those who would divide up the world into racial groups with the so-called Aryan race at the top of an artificial hierarchy.

Watching my mom interact with different others was instructive as well, in that she treated all others as her peers in the universe. Not only did she give me the information verbally, but she demonstrated in her encounters with others how vital it was to seek peer relationships. She was not bound by the typical lines of demarcation, and in her rejection of those barriers taught me to ignore them as well. Someone asked the comedian Eddie Murphy if he were anti-Semitic, and his reply: "I don't have time to divide white people up into little groups." In truth, none of us have the right, the authority, the scientific basis, nor the social, cultural, political or spiritual mandate to divide any of us into little groups. We are all part of the collective. As a psychologist it has been my goal to create a professional practice that is informed by these principles I learned from my mom.

Just how does one incorporate and use tenets of inclusion, and just what is meant by embracing and honoring difference? Let me share with you an episode from my days in practice in the Napa Valley. I begin with my colleague, a Chinese American who, upon learning of my desire to open a psychology practice, responded with what seemed to be the ultimate non sequitur. He said: "But, it's a long way to Vallejo!" I was too new to the region to have ascertained that Vallejo is a city populated by a large number of black people. My colleague could not mentally grasp the idea that I intended to work with the people who lived nearby. In any case, I did just that. I opened an office in the St. Helena Hospital located in Deer Park, California, adjacent to the city of St. Helena. My colleague was silent but no doubt in wonderment at what must have seemed to him to be the beginning of my state of dementia.

A few weeks into the practice my secretary scheduled an appointment with a new client. On the day she arrived, I was seated at my desk in the inner office, and the secretary rang to inform me that the new client was present. I asked her to send the client in and waited for the new face to appear. As I looked toward the door, I saw a woman literally stop as if she had run into a plate-glass window. Her forward momentum was arrested, and her mouth dropped open. She looked at me squarely, and said in the calmest voice possible, "I don't think I will be able to work with you because you are black." I arose from my chair, invited her in, and suggested she take the seat just opposite my desk. She did so, and in minutes we were communicating as if we had been lifelong acquaintances.

The secret? No secret really. I treated her as my peer, and demonstrated that I was not interested in judging her for her thoughts or opinions about me, a black person. I assumed from her opening remark that she had developed very negative ideas about black people in general. This was in fact confirmed during the time we worked together. She was a person of Greek ancestry, and had not interacted with any black people on more than a surface level for her entire life. She did, however, have notions about who black people were, and how important it was for her to stay far removed from them. It is safe to say at this point that she was probably able to alter those notions, subsequent to what turned out to be a successful clinical intervention.

And that brings us back to the idea of the importance of self as a tool in this arena of multicultural psychology. A less aware self may have bristled at the audacity of someone to speak in such a manner. What right have you to define all black people according to some racist thought process? Just who do you think you are anyway?

But the aware self knows in advance that when others speak, what is heard is a self-description, nothing at all to do with you, the hearer. The aware self knows also that hearing certain words or phrases may have the power to trigger emotions which may lead to defensive actions. It is a wise self who prepares in advance for any such happenstance. Years ago, during the time I was a Boy Scout, I was impressed by the Scout motto: "Be prepared." I didn't know at the time how vital that phrase would be for me as a professional clinician, but it has relevance now as much or more than it did then.

Last year, my wife and I were playing tennis at the Cal Tech tennis courts in Pasadena. We are members of the Cal Tech athletic program which gives us access to the courts. On this particular day, we were playing on Court 6. This piece of information is important for you to understand the series of events that led to my being triggered emotionally. There are a total of eight courts, and they are arranged in sets of two, 1&2, 3&4, 5&6, 7&8. I saw a young white man approach courts 1&2. He bypassed those courts as he also made his way past courts 3&4, and stopped outside the fence surrounding Court 6 where we were playing.

He yelled out: "Hey, do you have cards?" I was instantly triggered. Fortunately, I realized what had just happened, and I immediately took steps to calm down; I took a deep breath and walked slowly toward the young man. With each step in his direction, I felt my emotional temperature gauge drop significantly. What he didn't know, and what some of you have not yet figured out either, was that he had tapped into something primal inside me. My reaction had more to do with overt challenges from racist white men well before this young man was born. He was simply and merely symbolic of countless encounters that had left emotional scars on my psyche. But as I said, I realized all of this and took steps to spare him the unmitigated wrath that might have been unleashed. It was helpful that he was behind the chain link fence!

As I approached him, I made eye contact and held his gaze. I spoke in an even-toned voice: "Do you have a card?" He was flustered, and tried to find some form of identification, anything that would verify his legitimacy—give me some proof that he had the right to question me. He could find nothing, and finally pointed to the Cal Tech insignia on his jacket. That, I said, could have been purchased at the athletic store; it held little meaning for me. But, I was willing to grant him the authority to monitor the courts.

"What troubled me," I said, "was your approach. It would have been much better for both of us if you had said, 'Good morning, my name is ____________, and I am charged with the responsibility of making sure all players here are bona fide members of the athletic club.' I will show you our cards; but I want you to go back to the courts you passed on the way here and check the cards of those players, as well as the cards of players on 5, 7, and 8."

He did so, and we continued to play, but the ambiance had been shattered. What had started out as a delightful interlude had become an "incident"—a new and different marker in time and space for that day in our lives.

There have been other such unpleasant encounters for me; and I am certain that if we were to poll the group present today, we could collect enough like stories to fill reams of paper. The point is, however, that this is part of the reality of a multicultural world. How we deal with that reality is our focus.

Earlier in this talk, I referred to the ideas of critical mass and commitment. If enough of us build selves that are solidly grounded—infused with ideas that go far beyond the narrowly defined status quo of our social, political, and cultural worlds—and, if we commit to using self in ways that promote peer-to-peer existence, the changes that we will see will truly amaze us. When we learn to say, "Hello, my name is ____________," to anybody who crosses our path, the change begins.

The starting point is easy to define. It is what comes next that has me waiting with bated breath. My hope is that whatever is step two in that encounter will operate to impel both parties toward mutual understanding and renewed commitment to the highest ideals of human potentials and possibilities.

As you continue to learn about the use of self as a clinical tool, keep in mind that you have all you need already. Your task is to develop the necessary awareness that will allow you to use this tool with efficacy. Spare no energy in your quest to become excellent practitioners. The world awaits you!

Life in the 21st Century: Coping With A Legacy of Racism[3]

Paper presented at Annual Dinner hosted by Altadena-Pasadena Chapter, NAACP, Dodd Hall, Los Angeles, California

November 19, 1989

In preparation for a recent talk presented to members of the Title I Parents National Coalition, I read one of their handouts and learned that one of the aims of the founding group was to help other parents become involved in the education of their children. It occurred to me that perhaps a more appropriate objective would have been to point out to parents how they are already involved in this process: that their children learn from them whether they are actively promoting the learning or not.

And then, reflecting on the theme for their conference, "How Parents and Families can Communicate Better with Teachers," I thought, if parents are not fully engaged in directing the course of learning for their children, we will most certainly enter the new century just as confused as we are now.

We enter the universe, and immediately we are saddled with a vast storehouse of ignorance. If we as parents do not confront this reality, and urge our children to do the same, the storehouse of ignorance increases, and we miss opportunities to learn about life and how to live it. You see, our primary task, the first item on everyone's agenda, is that of overcoming ignorance, of learning what there is to be known. Parents have the double responsibility of being in charge of their own learning as well as that of children entrusted to their care.

As an example, considering our topic today, each one of us is faced with the task of learning about racism and its impact in our lives. Then we must communicate to our children what racism is all about. Obviously, if we fail at the first task, we cannot properly assume the second. It is incumbent upon us to confront racism as it exists inside ourselves, and to figure out what to do with the information we gather in the process.

In a real sense, as we close out the 20th Century, we have gone beyond racism. We have reached a point in our ability to think, in our accumulation of useful knowledge, that allows us to envision life without the onerous burden of racist ideology. Tragically, only a few of us are willing to let go of this color-coded way of relating to others.

Let us take a look at the origins of racism in this country to see if we can ferret out the reasons why it continues to be such an attractive option among the vast array of choices related to coping with difference. Racism has been defined in numerous ways, but for our discussion, I will suggest that it is an ideology based on the assumption that one group in society is superior to all other groups in that same society. This ideology, this way of thinking, is founded on the notion of race—the notion that all of humanity can be divided into observable populations distinguished by physical traits. Those who accept this notion tell us further that race is a biological fact; that we can determine one's racial category by applying some scientific criteria.

I need not point out the absurdity of this way of thinking, how race as a social, economic, or political concept is much more tenable; yet, historically, race and racism have been concepts virtually unchallenged in the minds of most U.S. citizens. Race is a product of history, not of nature. It follows from this logic that racism is also a product of history.

Racism was used as a means of justifying the theft of land

from Native Americans, and later as a way of explaining how it was permissible to force Africans to work without pay so that others might enrich themselves. This ideology of racism was promulgated by European Americans who gained great advantage from doing so. As they seized control of the means of communication, scientific inquiry, education, government, and religious instruction, these early racists were undaunted in their efforts to weave the threads of racism into the whole cloth of United States society.

In his recent work, *We the People: and Others,* Benjamin Ringer carefully documents an American duality described by the title of his work. He puts forth the idea that America, from its inception, has harbored two camps: "we the people," meaning white Americans, and the "others," meaning people of color.

Ringer is persuasive in his argument that it has been tension between these two camps that has characterized the historical development of this nation. As colonialists, the English subjected the nonwhites with whom they came into contact to violence, force, and fraud; and they subjugated, killed, or drove them off. The Indians, for example, were overwhelmed by force of arms, deprived of their land and resources, and treated as a conquered subject or inhuman enemy. Blacks were involuntarily brought into the colonies to work as slaves, and treated as a dehumanized chattel property.

You may have searched the historical records for yourselves and discovered already the extent to which European Americans have been willing to promote this doctrine of white supremacy. If so, you have been appalled as I have been in my own search for information about the origins of this onerous way of thinking. If you have not yet opened the pages of history to be informed about this world we share, I would encourage you to do so, especially as we contemplate life in a new century. It is by learning the lessons of the past that we avoid making the mistakes of the past. The ideology of racism has been used to rationalize barbaric behavior; it has remained a strong, viable force.

Charles Lawrence, writing in the *Stanford Law Review* in 1987, has this to say: Racism in America is much more complex than either the conscious conspiracy of a power elite or the simple delusion of a few ignorant bigots. It is part of our common historical experience and, therefore, a part of our culture. It arises from the assumptions we have learned to make about the world, ourselves, and others as well as from the patterns of our fundamental social activities.

None of this explains, however, why racism is the ideology of choice for so many contemporary Americans. Perhaps it is a basic inertia, an unwillingness to expend the energy required to reverse a pattern of culture. Or, it may be that greed, desire for power, and feelings of superiority loom much larger than notions of egalitarian co-existence.

As the recipients of this legacy of racism, we have learned to think in racial terms. We see self and each other as members of racial groups. One of the biggest barriers to our ability to communicate with each other is the tendency to evaluate on the basis of racial stereotypes.

In his most recent book, *Strangers from a Different Shore*, Ronald Takaki, Professor of Ethnic Studies at UC Berkeley, underscores how even a so-called positive stereotype can be extremely detrimental to the thought processes of those who refuse to think beyond the surface. He explodes the myth of the "model minority" that has developed to explain the so-called success of Asian Americans. A very cursory review of American institutions of education, finance, business, and industry reveal a curious absence of Asian Americans among the ranks of management and administrative personnel. Takaki writes, "though they are highly educated, Asian Americans are generally not present in positions of executive leadership and decision making." Further, anti-Asian sentiment is clearly on the rise in this country. Making it to "model minority" status is no passport to equality and freedom from racist attack.

Psychological confusion and bewilderment is another aspect of the legacy of racism. In this regard, I think of those writers who have combined their efforts to define racism out of existence, and to put in its place a theoretical formulation that depends for its substance upon the notion that people of color are victims of their own inability to rid themselves of, as Shelby Steele puts it, an "inferiority anxiety." Although they may not use the same terminology, other African-American scholars including Tom Sowell, Walter Williams, William Wilson, and Glenn Loury have presented arguments supporting this same theme.

What binds these kindred spirits together is a mutual acceptance of the idea that racism is no longer a major factor in the lives of African Americans. Wilson writes:

"It would be shortsighted to view the traditional forms of racial segregation and discrimination as having essentially disappeared in contemporary America... However, in the economic sphere, class has become more important than race in determining black access to power and privilege."

Steele puts it this way: "Certainly there is still racial discrimination in America, but I believe that the unconscious replaying of our oppression is now the greatest barrier to full equality."

It is puzzling, on the one hand, how these learned gentlemen could come to such conclusions. But, as I consider the psychological dimensions, the inherent need to belong to the body politic, the desire to be part of a viable world of meaningful action, the sheer agony of knowing that forces outside one's own control can determine fate and future, then it is not so hard to understand their plea.

The harsh reality is that racism exists. No matter how much these voices would have us turn away from that reality, it remains. These scholars are attempting to make sense out of a nonsensical entity. Blaming self, or blaming the victim, is not a new strategy, but one that does not suffice even though it comes dressed in new rhetoric. Racism robs us of the ability to see beyond a we/they dichotomy. It legitimizes thought patterns that color all of life as either black or white.

As creatures of this universe we need other, competing ways of thinking. In this very important sphere of our existence, human relationships, we nurture an etiquette based on racism that, when followed slavishly, leads us further away from that grand vision that would have us see each other as beings worthy of positive consideration. Racism can and does distort our language to the extent that we constantly reaffirm principles that negate the value of human beings.

Language is the basic coin of transaction between people in any culture or society, and when distortions abound, language becomes a tool of oppression. It is through the use of words that we fashion reality, create a context for our existence. If we use words that support the superiority of one group over others, we help to build a reality that mitigates against the full and complete development of all people. Your vocabulary, if not structured according to humanitarian ideals, can help perpetuate thought patterns that erode those ideals.

Further, what you say to yourself often can spell the difference between success and failure in any area of life. Twenty-four hours a day you play a movie in your own head, you write the script, you supply the dialogue. If you have not gone beyond racism, that movie can only be rated double X, not fit for human consumption.

Several years ago, when the late Bart Giamatti was president of Yale University, I listened to him explain how admissions worked at Yale. Along with my daughter, I attended a session chaired by Giamatti in which he stated that it would be less than candid of him to leave us with the impression that all students were selected on the basis of merit alone. He told us that applicants who showed unusual athletic ability, or whose families had contributed large sums of money to Yale, or whose parents had graduated from Yale, were given priority in the admissions pool.

Some would say that this kind of affirmative action is a program that has no place in American society. Those who support this point of view often extol the virtues of meritocracy, and define affirmative action as a project designed to give unfair advantages to those who do not merit them. Affirmative action is not about giving anything. It is about doing whatever is necessary to insure that all qualified persons have opportunity to maximize their potential.

In a campus newspaper editorial written last year by students from the Claremont Colleges, we find evidence of the twisted thinking about affirmative action. The two writers conclude that standards will be lowered if we follow affirmative-action principles. During that same time period, a cartoon appeared in UCLA's *Daily Bruin* wherein a rooster explained his presence on campus by saying that he was there as a result of affirmative action. These two examples are not isolated incidents. They underscore the depth of racist ideation among the citizens of this country. This legacy of racism that we lug inexorably toward the new century threatens to pollute yet another generation.

The most salient question for me is whether or not we are willing to pay the cost of eradicating, entirely, any and all racist thought and action. From a psychological point of view, it is essential that individuals choose to confront self: develop high-level self-awareness about our universe in ways that enhance the well-being of self and all others—a rather heady state of affairs about which I am only occasionally optimistic. And yet, a very necessary task, because it is prerequisite to the more important assignment of tackling institutional racism.

The new century deserves an educated corps of dedicated, politically minded, socially alert, and personally committed citizens who will identify racism and its perpetrators without reservation. We must learn to recognize that the elimination of racism requires education of the highest order; political surgery that results in cutting out of office those who would maintain a racist posture; social activism that demonstrates to a complacent electorate that they must vote into office only those who will vow to end racist practices; the willingness to confront even your own kin if they espouse racist ideals.

Will any of this take place in the year 2000 and thereafter? My gut feeling informs me that only a few people will explore this issue with any lasting commitment. My reading of history suggests that we have a long, troublesome road ahead before significant changes occur.

I say this with full awareness that there are those among us who believe that we have reached the promised land of racial equality. They point to the civil-rights laws and the economic gains made by some people of color as proof that we have overcome racism. And even though I will reiterate that technically, we have gone beyond racism, realistically, on a day-to-day basis, we are mired today as deep as we have been since Plymouth Rock took its place as a point of reference in our convoluted history.

Coping with racism demands the best we can give. If indeed, we are to make of this country what it has the potential to be, we must insist on having only the very best quality for our relationships, our families, our organizations, our industries, our hopes, dreams, expectations, and desires.

As a young person growing up in the American South, the most frequent admonition from significant adults in my life was, "Boy, get your education." What that meant at the time, or what it means now is open to speculation. But, in any case, we need to look at the charge as one that would propel us toward something higher and nobler than that which we now have. In today's language, perhaps, I would say to you, commit yourself, fully and completely, to the task of learning all that you can learn. Then, put it to use in the service of helping fellow African Americans cope with this legacy of racism that will, without doubt, follow us into the next century.

Education: A Power Tool for the 21st Century

Article published in African American Perspectives Magazine

February 2007

Not too long ago, I saw a tee shirt with a message that caught my attention. On the front of the shirt was this question: "So you think education is expensive?" And on the back of that same shirt, these words: "Try Ignorance!" A bit of homespun folk wisdom perhaps, but there is enough here to give one pause. An educated populace would surely be less demanding of the public treasury than those who opt for a life of ignorance. And it is not only the economic concerns that pose threats to the safety and well-being of our society.

Think about the consequences of living in a world with fellow citizens who cannot read or write, who cannot compute simple sums, or who cannot understand elementary directions for using the various and sundry items we routinely employ in the course of a day's activities? Needless to say, it would not be the most desirable situation.

I count myself fortunate to have been in the first-grade classroom run by Miss Waugh, who told us that we must become executives in charge of our own education; that we must take executive responsibility for learning the lessons we needed to learn. She led by example. Her life was one dedicated to learning, and perhaps in a different world she would have been called not teacher, but learner. Watching her inspired me to follow her advice and counsel.

It was in her classroom, too, that I learned my definition of education. According to her, education is defined as knowing about the available options. Terse, certainly, but pithy, meaningful, filled with possibilities far beyond our ability to comprehend. In the universe there are billions of options available to us, but generally we know very few of them. An educated person is one who knows more of those options than the average man on the street.

What makes this definition even more poignant is that human beings can only choose among the options that exist; we cannot create anything, nor can we destroy anything. We can, for instance, participate in the transformation of a solid substance such as a piece of paper by igniting it, and then watching it become gas and ash; but we cannot destroy the energy it contains. There is little need here to explain our lack of ability to create; that one seems self-evident.

The power of choice, however, is not well understood by the masses; but when we define education in terms of knowing the available options, it begins to make more sense. Education is without doubt a power tool for the 21st Century; it is the power of choice in action. Alvin Toffler divided up all of our known history into 20-year lifetimes, and concluded that most of what we know as the "prevailing body of knowledge" was discovered in the last few lifetimes. Put another way, our options have increased geometrically in very recent times. The "educated" man of yesteryear would not be so labeled in today's complex universe. The range of choices have so far outstripped his experience that he would be lost, uncertain even about what his choices represented or related to.

It is interesting to note in this discussion that our group of nine chose to go to Central High School in 1957 only because the option of going there prior to 1957 was not on our radar screens; it was not on anybody's screen! And, I think it is fair to say, even with an opportunity present, nothing happens unless the person or persons who know about the opportunity are willing to exercise the right of choice. And we all saw what happened in the wake of our choice to enroll at Central High. The opposition would have preferred that we remain in ignorance, unaware of the expanded range of choices; or perhaps more to the point, that we would refuse to exercise our right to choose.

But education does not just mean that we locate newer, bigger, and better options, but that we do indeed exercise those options, and build stronger foundations to support an even more complete body of knowledge, a storehouse of prodigious proportions. Yes, education is the power tool, but we have to learn how to use the tool with efficiency and expertise. One bias of mine that rears its head at this point is that I don't believe that individuals can claim to be educated outside the context of meaningful human relationships.

This year, 2007, the Little Rock Nine Foundation will award nine scholarships to graduating high-school seniors. In addition to the financial award, each recipient will be assigned to a mentor who will engage with him or her in an ongoing relationship. In this case, the mentors will be members of the Little Rock Nine. The well-worn adage "each one, teach one" comes to mind here. In their second year of college, this group of nine awardees will be asked to mentor the scholarship recipients of 2008. If all goes as planned, subsequent years will find this chain extended until we have a virtual nation of students and mentors, all proving the efficacy of relationship as a component of true education.

I am utterly convinced of the need to be in such relationships at all levels of our society. One of the things I despaired about at Central High was that very few, if any, white students were willing to build relationships with the nine of us. The need for dialogue was apparent; but the allegiance to the myth of white superiority was too strong, and promoted with such vigor that any possible opportunities for cerebral interchanges were lost amidst the visceral explosions of racist ideology.

Today we live in what many describe as a global village. We are privileged to be in close contact with people from every corner of the known universe. If we continue to hide behind the grossly incorrect notion of a viable racial hierarchy, and if we cling to belief systems that separate and divide rather than lead toward policies of inclusion, we violate the village law. True education lets us in on the secret of including others in our lifespace, of treating all others in the universe as our peers. As we interact without evaluating or judging each other, as we share what we know, the benefit is obvious: all of us gain access to more options.

The power of education lies not so much in what it does for the individual, but what happens to the entire community. The educated individual understands that he or she exists, not in isolation, but in the context of billions of others, all of whom seek to find ways to maximize the potential that is theirs at birth. By building viable relationships, by sharing knowledge, by operating together as peers, citizens of the world village can demonstrate the power of education not only in the 21st Century, but can leave a legacy for all those who are born into future generations.

Seeking to Explain Clarence[4]

June 20, 2001

There was, at the outset, hesitation, a twinge of doubt that explanations could be found. In truth, is such a quest honorable, or necessary, I asked myself. Yes, yes, yes, the answer came. Erase the edges of doubt and know that you must, at least, make the attempt to shed revealing light on this man and his mission. What, after all, is it that drives a man to such machinations?

There is a general and specific need to know. General, in the sense that others may aspire to similar heights of fantasy, and Clarence could prove to be a useful prototype—a model for comparison and comparative analysis. Specific in that this man could prove to be even more dangerous than he appears, and that calls for information of a defensive, life-preserving sort. To know is to be fortified against the possible eventuality in whatever guise it may appear. And even if it proves to be an act of specious preparation, the calming effect in the moment cannot be discounted. Forewarned, as they say, and all that goes with that adage.

But what is it, you may say, that begs such an explanation? Here, I must confess a dilemma. To me the thing is clearly displayed, the images sharp, and fashioned in bold relief on the inner surfaces of my mind. My dilemma is that I may fall into a thought process that tells me that you, the reader, share my perceptions. Given that, I might fail to describe adequately the full and true nature of the beast. Forgive me if I omit important details, but know that these supporting bits of information do solemnly exist, and are available for your review. So, where do we start?

Perhaps the psychological underpinning would give us a foothold to begin this journey into the mind and manner of Clarence. It is my considered opinion that he can best be described as one who has seen and experienced the harsh reality of being black in these United States of America, and has rejected that reality out of hand. In its stead he has created a linguistic and behavioral fiction to which he is joined in the manner of metal fused to metal. Makeshift, yet intended to be permanent.

This pseudo-reality contains all of the elements one might expect to find in a utopian version of a country now dedicated to whiteness and the protocols that support notions of white supremacy. In this made-up version, in the world of Clarence, all people are treated equally in all spheres of our existence. There is no racism; hence no need for such outmoded artifacts as affirmative action or government-contract set asides. There are no restrictions on upward mobility, and all the glass ceilings have been shattered. Using self as the barometer, Clarence proves, by sitting silently on the bench, that anybody can do anything. In this, dare I say, brave new world, Clarence acts as if, and decides that it is, indeed, true.

He is not alone in opting for this seemingly safe, snug, psychological harbor. Though their numbers are not legion, others do exist, and they espouse views similar to those embraced by Clarence. Ward Connerly, Shelby Steele, and Thomas Sowell are names that come swiftly to mind, and other faces tumble about in the recesses of my brain; but in consideration of my own mental well being, I choose not to bring them too sharply into focus. Too much at once could prove to be deleterious; I approach this enterprise with a certain caution.

In one sense this could all be charged to certain psychological defense accounts. In order to navigate successfully a known hostile terrain, often actors will simply conjure up screenplays for life that offer starring roles. No bit parts or cameo slots for this crowd. And even if one of this ilk has the misfortune of being pulled over by one or two of those stalwart blue-clad guardians of the public peace, forced up against the wall, and ordered to "spread 'em!" it was not, in this instance, a case of racial profiling. No, this was simply an isolated case of mistaken identity in an otherwise well-functioning universe. Do, indeed, charge it up to psychological defense; preserve the fiction, but don't by any means give credence to those voices crying out from that Jurassic era when racist ideology prevailed.

In extreme cases there exists as well an additional piece of this puzzle that is indeed pernicious in character. That is the wholesale rejection of blackness in favor of whiteness in any and all of its forms. The overt manifestation of this aspect may very well include the acquisition of a white spouse or partner, although this is, in itself, not prima facie evidence of an adherence to the fictional reality described above. Although, for some, such an alliance is seen to be a necessary element in the overall schema, it alone is not sufficient to declare the one so attached to be a disciple of Clarencism.

No, there has to be a plethora of evidence including, but not limited to, seeking out venues peopled primarily by so-called white people; using myriad concoctions to whiten the skin (and you thought Michael was an outlier?); campaigning and voting for Republican candidates for public office; shunning food and/or music too closely related to the experience of being black in this society; but not, I repeat not, listening to country music. I mean, there are limits here! Even among the ranks of those who gather beneath the banner of "We are all just Americans," there are those who cannot abide the nasal twang and the sad tales of broken homes, alcoholic binges, pickup trucks, lonely train whistles and failed romances.

It is, however, the covert aspects of this that cause the hairs on the back of my neck to rise, and the blood to course through my veins in an agitated acceleration. I know the signs that bespeak a way of thinking in support of this fictional reality. I see the excessive doting on progeny springing from the loins of the carefully chosen spouse, and know that this is rooted in the belief that white, after all, is better.

Woe be unto the child, however, who tumbles out of the womb in possession of genetic ties to those hanging on the other side of the family tree. An unbridled tongue in the service of combating efforts toward legal, educational, employment, and social equity for black people gets its energy from a held belief that blackness is most clearly associated with severely limited ability and/or laziness.

What good then could possibly be accomplished by supporting compensatory programs? Support for law and order initiatives that spill out of legislatures over the length and breadth of this nation, however, can be offered because of the conviction that criminality is genetic among black Americans. The most frightening thing about these belief systems is that they fuel decisions at so many varied levels, most of which we are not privy to until it is too late to counter their impact. Also, those who hold these notions dear become vulnerable to the nefarious schemes of white racists who need spokespersons of color to carry their venomous rhetoric into communities largely populated by black people. As a trusted friend of mine said recently, "Some black people will carry water for white people for little or no compensation."

Ward Connerly is the foremost current-century example of his sort of thing in California. He has agreed to be the poster child for anti-affirmative-action efforts, and has proven to be tireless in his push to dismantle programs that have proven to be beneficial to people of color. Part of the craziness of this drama is that Clarence himself was, as was Ward, at one time, a beneficiary of affirmative-action programs. Go figure. And did I mention Ward's wife? Well, you see, there you go.

There are, of course, other options available. Denial is not the only way to confront this hurtful reality we face. Resistance is a distinct possibility. Resisting the impulse to give in to the forces arrayed against us, resisting the tendency to favor whiteness over blackness, resisting as a way of life. It is not even necessary to become a fighter (although there are positions open for stalwart warriors); it is enough to become an active thinker. A commitment to think seriously about the issues would mark you as one altogether unlike Clarence, yes. But more than that: such cerebral activity would allow you to unearth the miasmic slag festering just beneath this thin veneer of civility we stand upon.

Guerilla warfare from inside the corporate boardroom or the academic senate is also an option to be considered. It is not as if Clarence is without instruction about these alternative choices. The unfortunate reality is that he is simply not interested in the goals and objectives portended by these change-oriented positions. Wedded to his ersatz world and all of its various support systems, he is satisfied to guard the edges of his virtual paradise. But why would a black man, after sifting through all of the possible responses to a society bent on defining him into nothingness, opt to join forces with the perpetrators of this gross ignominy?

The answer lies at the heart of this enigma. Peering into the depths, we find a timid, frightened, self-doubting soul who is not convinced that his black skin is the proper covering for a real person. To my knowledge, it was *not* Clarence who said, "I'm not having any nappy headed babies," or, "I would never marry anyone with skin that dark." But I would not be surprised to find Clarence on the sidelines cheering madly in support of those who did, or who would give voice to such sentiments.

Perception is the means by which we give substance and meaning to reality. Nothing makes any sense whatsoever until we impose definition upon it. Face-to-face with himself, gazing at his mirror image, Clarence engages in a mental metamorphosis to create an aura of whiteness. This fictional reality is bolstered by the very real chalk-white face of his wife whose image can be seen flickering in the background, giving credence to his cherished thought, "I'm just as good as any other white man."

Sadly Clarence does not realize that he has no need whatsoever to compare himself with any other man, black or white. His fascination with this aspect of being makes it highly unlikely that he will ever be able to render judgments with any degree of objectivity. He is at the center of his world—his white, non-racist, edenic world. And there is no room for any of us, unless we happen to share his convoluted notions. My fear is that too many of us do![5]

Regarding Daisy: Thoughts Drafted in Anticipation of a Celebration of Life[6]

November 5, 1999

Beyond expectation, and beyond belief for many who would have relegated all black people to the end of every line, Daisy Bates stood her ground and spoke words of truth without flinching. In the face of stalwart bigotry, eye to eye with those who refused to see her humanity, this courageous woman said no to racism; no to all the practices that worked to deny equal educational opportunities to black children in Little Rock. Unyielding in her demands that the Little Rock Nine be admitted to Central High School, Daisy Bates was willing to place her own life on the line of demarcation drawn by the governor himself. Unmoved by the threats of violence or the violent acts that targeted her person and her property, Daisy Bates continued to push against the onerous walls of separation that excluded black citizens from the main corridors of political, economic, educational, and social activity in this city.

It was in large measure the vision of Daisy Bates that made it possible for us, the Little Rock Nine, to confront, on a daily basis, the unmitigated hatred of those who tried mightily to ban us from the classrooms at Central High. Her support and encouragement undergirded our own resolve to defy the forces arrayed against us.

As we gather here to salute this warrior for justice and equality, let us be reminded of the context in which she fought her good fight. In that time, in this place, it was not a popular choice to defend boldly the rights of black people. It was then that Emmett Till could be so cruelly murdered in the neighboring State of Mississippi; it was then that Martin Luther King, Jr., was being tested severely in the neighboring State of Alabama; it was then that Orval Faubus filled the air with racist rhetoric here in our own State of Arkansas. Yet, it was then as well that Daisy Bates walked the talk of freedom for all; strode confidently forward, keenly aware of the dangers she faced, but resolute in her determination to see the walls of segregation come tumbling down.

Yes, it is fitting and proper that we pay respect to her memory today. Daisy Bates was indeed one of the brighter lights of her time. Turning her face to the evils of racism, she sought to bring us all out of the darkness that impeded our progress toward a just society. May we all commit to continuing that quest as we act collectively to keep the vision of Daisy Bates alive in the 21st Century.

Philander Smith College Remarks[7]

Saturday, September 27, 1997

As I stand in this spot, I can see down Izard Street where I lived as a young boy growing up in Little Rock. Coming to the campus at Philander Smith College was on my playtime agenda as my friends and I climbed these steps and slid down these banisters. I am on familiar ground today. Later, Philander Smith was to provide much-needed services to me and my eight colleagues when we were denied entrance to Central High School in September, 1957. During the three-week period as we awaited the outcome of the legal wrangling over states' rights versus federal rights, Philander Smith College faculty and students tutored us in the high school subjects being taught to our future Central High classmates.

From these dedicated educators and scholars we heard the same litany that had been communicated to us by teachers at Gibbs Elementary, Stephens Elementary, Dunbar Junior High School, and Horace Mann High. They told us in words chosen carefully to accentuate the message that education was important, and that excellence was the expectation. They continued to do this for the entire academic year of 1958-59 as well, when all Little Rock public high schools were closed in the name of segregation forever, and African American students were in need of educational resources.

Earlier today, I spoke to a group of Philander Smith students and urged them to take the educational process seriously, to resist the impulse to follow pathways that might lead them away from the center of the educational arena, and to accept the mantle of learner with all of its attendant requirements, the foremost one of which is the choice to commit at the fifth level: to do whatever it takes to succeed.

The first level of commitment is embodied in the reply, "I'll think about it." Not much commitment even hinted at here. Following is the second level, "I'll try," which is not much better that the first. The next level, "I'll do what I can," seems to promise more, but it too is empty of substance. The fourth level describes the degree of commitment given by the legalist, the one who follows the letter of the law. This person will do only that which is required, not an iota more.

It is the fifth level that demands total involvement. It was a fifth-level commitment that we took to Central High School. This commitment enabled us to accept the restrictions placed upon us as we sought to educate ourselves in an unfriendly, hostile environment.

The school officials demanded that we, the Little Rock Nine, not participate in extracurricular activities while we were in school, as a condition of our enrollment. The manifest reason was that our safety could not be insured. Given that we had the backing of the 101st Airborne Division of the United States Army, I am forced to conclude that there was probably a latent rationale for this decision. And one such possible explanation would be that, by keeping us segregated within this milieu, we would not reap the intangible benefits that accrue to those who are free to form whatever associations they choose, associations that might enhance the developmental process.

The development of contacts that extend beyond the high-school corridors, and which could translate into admission to better colleges, jobs with better potential for advancement, the transfer of information necessary for the building of substantive social networks—all of this and more might result from the unfettered association that an open society demands—the kind of affirmative action that has always existed for white Americans, but which has been systematically denied to black Americans.

In his book, *The Birth and Death of Meaning*, Ernest Becker penned these words which have become one of my favorite phrases to quote: “It is the task of culture to provide each and every individual with the firm conviction that he or she is an object of primary value in a world of meaningful action.”

This community failed in its obligation to me in 1957. Finally, after military force was applied, I was offered a shadow, but little substance. Years ago, a friend of mine said that the taste of honey is bitter when niggardly given by the lily-white hand that beats you; I think he was on to something.

In the past few days, several of us have made public statements about the need to focus on access as we think about the integration of schools. I would like to reiterate that, and to add that we are talking about total access; we want it all. We don’t want just a taste. In order to facilitate the healthy growth and development of African American children in this multiracial, multiethnic, multilingual society, we need to give them the chance to communicate and interact with everybody else.

The same is true for white youngsters as well. It would be unfortunate if our remarks were misconstrued in any way to suggest that we were against the desegregation of schools. The Little Rock Nine stands firmly committed to the desegregation of schools. We know that Little Rock’s schools remain under federal orders to desegregate; this has been the case since 1956, 41 years ago. We are aware of the school district’s latest proposal to have the Eighth Circuit Court of Appeals approve their revision of the desegregation plan which would remove court supervision by the school year 2001. To that I would simply say, if what the Little Rock School District plans to do has merit—if, in fact, the plan is based on principles of equality for all students regardless of color or ethnicity—the results will stand the scrutiny of any overseeing body even beyond the year 2001. Obviously, the step we took in 1957 has not been followed by the necessary additional steps to insure that all school children in this city have maximum opportunity to realize the potential that is theirs.

In the exhibition in the state capitol rotunda that presents the rich history of Dunbar Junior High School, there is a section where one can read about the language routinely printed on diplomas awarded to graduating students. It is written that the holder of this diploma qualifies for entrance into Little Rock Central High School; but the rules of segregation were so well-entrenched that no students graduating from Dunbar ever concluded that attendance there was possible.

To structure a society in such a manner robs all of its citizens of opportunities to grow and prosper in the truest sense. For many African Americans, leaving Little Rock was the only viable pathway to academic and professional success. The tragedy of that reality is reflected in the disintegration of families, and the loss of social frameworks that would have included the formal and informal transfer of knowledge and information between and among African Americans at each end and along a wide continuum.

The security of having an established home base, with a loving extended family and a school system where you are cherished and expected to succeed, fits well with Becker's notion about the task of culture. If the Little Rock School District would like to move beyond the confines of restricted thinking into a realm of fifth-level commitment to the highest ideals, they can start using all available energy to figure out how to make Becker's idea real in the school system.

Jonathan Kozol, in his preface to *Death at an Early Age,* writes: The most pernicious thing an adult can do to a child is to meet him or her with minimal expectations—my paraphrase. When my own children were in grade school, they told me about a classmate whose parents had given her a dollar for each grade of A she earned. My reply was that since going to school was their main job, their primary chore, then they would owe me a dollar for each class in which they did not earn the grade of A. It was all about levels of expectations.

Sitting to my right is a man I met in 1987 when he was governor of Arkansas. I remember coming home to share with my wife that I had met a man who seemed to "get it." He appeared to understand this country's need to confront the issues of race and racism.

Now, as president, Bill Clinton has established a commission to explore the dynamics of race and racism, which I hope will lead us all to a fifth-level commitment to do whatever it takes to move this country beyond the narrow confines of racial prejudice and discrimination into the realm of peer relationships, where each person is honored and embraced without imposed conditions.

It is my expectation that we will indeed take the opportunity that is ours to structure a society for the 21st Century that offers all citizens the right to exist unfettered by the restrictions of racist ideology or its nefarious soul mate, the notion of white supremacy. Until each person is free to follow the pathways suggested by inherent potential, none of us are truly free.

The Ongoing Battle for Equality[8]

Op-ed in the Arkansas Democrat-Gazette

Thursday, September 25, 1997

According to some contemporary sources, the modern African-American civil rights struggle finds its genesis in Rosa Parks' refusal to give up her Montgomery, Alabama, bus seat to a white man on Dec. 1, 1955. From there, according to these same sources, the struggle moved to Little Rock, Arkansas in 1957 when nine black children needed the might of the 101st Airborne Division of the U.S. Army to enter the previously all-white Central High School.

Those events, as poignant as they were, did not occur in a vacuum. They were skirmishes in the ongoing battle for equality, fought tenaciously by enslaved Africans and African Americans throughout the history of this country. African slave men, women, and children worked amidst the cruelest conditions possible to build an economically strong America. At the same time, they sought full participation in the body politic as economic, political, and social equals. Many black people sacrificed their lives so that succeeding generations might have opportunities to maximize inherent potential without the threat of oppression.

When I consider that the battle rages still in 1997, I realize that I have no time for celebration. Time for reflection, yes; time for remembering the past so the future can be better informed, yes. But as Little Rock's schools remain under federal orders to desegregate, as affirmative action programs are being dismantled across the country, as statistics continue to show disproportionate distributions of income and wealth between racial groups, as one social barometer after another mirrors the dismal state of black people in the poorest strata of our economic hierarchy, it is clear to me that the time for celebration must be postponed.

This year, President Clinton appointed a seven-member commission to establish a national dialogue about things racial in the United States. This action I applaud, for it has long been my contention that the chief executive, by setting the necessary tone, can help this country find the will and commitment to end racism and the accompanying ideology of white supremacy. Despite our long history of fighting racist forces in education, employment, housing, transportation and other arenas, racism is very much alive in America. Despite the claims of some that classism, not racism, is the issue, we, African Americans, are faced with racist actions, attitudes and consequences every day of our existence. Starting a dialogue about this would serve to move us eventually from the visceral, reactionary stage to the level of cognitive engagement where we can develop strategies and mechanisms designed to eradicate every vestige of this consuming evil.

Many times I have been asked, "Don't you think we have made progress?" "Why do we still have to talk about racism?" "Can't we just be color-blind?" The questioners often are ready to celebrate what they see as stellar accomplishments and accuse me of being oversensitive and paranoid. I cannot, in good conscience, celebrate what some would label progress while so many of my fellow citizens of color remain oppressed.

In 1957 it was the goal of the Little Rock Nine to simply integrate a school. Our task was to take our places in the trenches to carry on the fight against forces that sought to relegate black people to the back of the bus, the back of the employment line, the back door. The task we all face today is not how to integrate schools but how to educate children of all ethnicities to think beyond the narrow confines of racist ideology. Our goal today is not to enrich ourselves so that we can encircle our necks with bands of South African gold but to invest the profits signaled by the rising Dow-Jones in ways that promote a vision for the 21st Century untrammeled by thoughts mired in our racist past.

As a young boy growing up in Little Rock, I was convinced that there must be a place somewhere that was not governed by the same rules that restricted my freedom in so many ways. As an adult, I have concluded that such a place can exist, but it will require concerted effort on the part of large numbers of American citizens. I have made the trek back to Little Rock this week to take part in the activities associated with the observance of the passage of 40 years since the initial desegregation of Central High. Some have talked of reconciliation as we remember those times and those events. I would simply remind those who speak in such terms that to be reconciled there must have been some friendship or harmony then in existence that can now be restored. Perhaps it would be more fruitful to talk about how we can confront the past and learn from it, and in so doing begin to build a future devoid of those structures created to place white people at the top of some mythical racial hierarchy.

We must remember that it was the governor of Arkansas, with the complicity of the people, who closed all of the public high schools in Little Rock during academic year 1958-59, an act so egregious that 40 years later, many who might have earned a high-school diploma have not done so. We must recall that it took yet another Supreme Court decision, *Cooper vs. Aaron,* to force the governor to open the schools. It was the voice of the White Citizen's Council that expressed so much open disdain for black citizens. It was the "average" white citizen, not some demented, deluded interloper, who filled the ranks of the mobs surrounding Central High.

We need to understand exactly how and why all of this happened so that it can be avoided in the future. In David Augsburger's insightfully written book, *Caring Enough to Confront,* we find his thesis that those who care enough will confront the issues pertinent to the relationship. If we care enough about the relationships between and among all the people of Little Rock, we have to confront the salient issues. And the chaos that engulfed us in 1957 has left us with a legacy of significant issues to be confronted.

I write these words from the fund of information that shapes my mental map, the guide I use to make sense of the world around me. In the ideal, I would write about some subject of compelling and general interest arising out of my unencumbered exploration of the universal terrain, but because of the reality we share, a reality marred by a plethora of racist decisions and consequences, I write in the name of civil rights for all people. It is my hope that we will have reasons to engage in the joyful celebration of full and complete freedom for black people in this country. Indeed, the time for celebration may come, but make no mistake, it has not yet arrived.

Remarks Delivered at the U.S. Postal Service

Announcement of the stamp commemorating
The Little Rock Nine[9]
Central High School, Little Rock, Arkansas
August 30, 2005

The United States Postal Service has long been an ally for black people in this country. For many upwardly mobile middle class black folk in Little Rock, a job with the Post Office was one of very few options available during a time when segregation was rigidly enforced. During my younger years in this city, working for the "government" or teaching in an all-black school were among the most viable choices; perhaps the only ones for people seeking to better themselves. It seems fitting, in light of this history, that today the Postal Service should honor the Little Rock Nine with this commemorative stamp.

In the collective consciousness, symbols loom large as a means of communicating sentiment, belief, or ideology. This symbolic postage stamp will take its place among many other such representative markers in time and space. It is clear that the choice to honor the Little Rock Nine in this manner communicates a far different message than did the banners, posters, and other means employed to convey a prevailing racist attitude in 1957. And, while symbols alone cannot alter thought or behavior, they do provide opportunity for reflection, time to reconsider, rethink, and perhaps alter ways of being in the universe.

A stamp with the imprimatur of the U. S. Postal Service and a symbolic image of the Little Rock Nine adds power to the notion that racism is on the wane. But, in truth, it is only those symbols that continue to reflect accurately the will of the people that retain their value to persuade or influence. It is my hope that this stamp will appreciate in its value as a means of convincing those committed to maintaining the status quo to see the efficacy of working toward the establishment of a society dedicated to the proposition that all people deserve access to opportunity.

On behalf of the Little Rock Nine, I say thank you to all who have labored to make this day possible—to all who believe in the promise of this country, to all who refuse to give in to the impulse of fear, to all who understand the true meaning of democracy. I look forward to the day when we can place our hands over our hearts and repeat those familiar words, "with liberty and justice for all," and discover that it is indeed a reality rather than just a dream for the future.

Letter to Philander Smith College Athletes[10]

Terrence J. Roberts, Ph.D.
P.O. Box 96
Pasadena, CA 91102

March 28, 2007

To the Athletes of Philander Smith College:

My first grade teacher told me that I should become the executive in charge of my own education; that I should take responsibility for finding out what I needed to learn and to learn it with some dispatch. She spoke a vital truth, and I heard the message; it came through loud and clear. Since that time I have been fascinated by the ever-growing world of possibilities that education unveils. You see, my simple definition of education is this: knowing the options available to you in the universe. I made an early executive decision to discover as many options as I could in this lifetime. And so I say to you, your life will be enriched, enhanced, completely exhilarating if you take executive responsibility for learning.

As a young black man in the hostile territory of Central High School in 1957, it was in part my choice to wear the executive mantle that made it possible for me to block out the extraneous noise in the system and concentrate my energies on learning. In truth, some of that learning included how to stay alive in the midst of those who would have preferred me dead, but even that anxiety-provoking reality was not enough to derail my focus. I knew even then that having access to more choices meant that I could eventually find ways to exercise my potential, unburdened by the machinations of those who cling to the false hope of whiteness, who worship at the altar of white racism, and who ultimately must face the reality of living in a world with people who see through the myth of white supremacy.

Go forth from Philander Smith College and seek the myriad, abundant choices in the universe. Explore every corner of the globe, seek truth wherever it can be found, build relationships that last, teach others about the things you have learned, and never forget that on any given day, the world is not complete until you make your own unique contribution.

Terrence J. Roberts, Ph.D.

Remarks at Facing History Benefit Dinner[11]

Los Angeles, California

March 6, 2002

Thank you and good evening. It is my pleasure to be with you to speak about the chaos that erupted in Little Rock, 1957, especially as it relates to us today in this year 2002. History in general offers each one of us an opportunity to learn the lessons spread out in the timeline before us. Little Rock, in particular, teaches us about what happens when we allow lines of demarcation to dictate how we relate to one another.

The Little Rock Nine sought access to an educational institution, a high school devoted, ostensibly, to the learning needs of the citizens of Little Rock. In fact, the school was reserved for white students only. The attempt to desegregate led to the eventual use of the United States military, which in itself is testimony to the fierceness of the opposition. Those opposed were so dedicated to the principles of segregation that it took the might of the United States army to dissuade them. One lesson for us is that when lines of separation become so important and so meaningful, people will resist erasure of those lines with all of their might.

The school year 1957-58 was filled with learning opportunities for the nine of us. We learned about ourselves and what it took to face continually the assaults on mind and body. We learned about the degree to which people imbued with the ideology of racism will pursue their chosen separatist goals. We learned that government and community leaders will use positions of power and authority to promote personal agendas. And we learned as well how history is often distorted to serve selfish purposes.

In this year 2002, as we look back at Little Rock, we can ferret out the lessons that have meaning and importance for us as we move forward into this 21st Century. We can see how the mythological construct of race was used as rationale for policies of discrimination in 1957, and commit to its complete erasure so that we are not troubled by it anymore. We can face the whole range of mythological concepts that fueled decision making then, and resolve to rid our community of any such debris in 2002.

This process is enhanced by the efforts of Facing History and Ourselves, as young people are encouraged to take executive responsibility for their own learning. When students at every level are challenged to review history and to employ the tools of critical analysis, they can create strong foundations for growth and development. They can learn how to ask important questions, and to sift through the varied answers with discerning minds which will lead them, eventually, to understandings that inform healthy choices for themselves and others.

As I listened earlier to one of the students speaking here tonight, I heard the statement "We're all connected." I hold that belief firmly. I often talk about being on "team universe," with an awareness that what each of us chooses to do matters to the rest of us, all of the time.

This is not a concept widely accepted, however. We need only look around the universe for examples to the contrary. War and destruction seem to be more than ever the options preferred by some members of our team.

Natalie Cole said, "You can make the world a better place." That too, I believe with some fervor. A few years ago, I attended a session conducted by a group known as Beyond War. Their philosophy is very simply this: Since we know how to fight already, since we have the firepower to blow up the globe, why not now turn our attention to matters of peace, not war.

At Central High School in Little Rock, the nine of us adopted a philosophy of nonviolence. We accepted the premise that fighting would not communicate what we really wanted to say. What we really wanted was to have an opportunity to educate ourselves at the neighborhood school, to say hello to fellow learners, and to find creative ways to enhance our mutual living space.

If each one of us would commit at the fifth level, if we would decide to do whatever it takes to change our world in positive ways, our collective energy would pay off in great dividends as we pursued goals of peace and harmony in our society. It will not happen by chance; it will not happen simply as a consequence of the passing of time, but it will happen if we choose to make it happen.

Scott Peck, the author of *The Road Less Traveled*, talks in yet another work about the need to build true community. He says that we live in pseudo-community at present: a space wherein we speak politely to each other, but make no real connections. To achieve true community, he goes on to say, we have to face the chaos of changing how we live with and among each other.

That is an invitation I very much want to accept. I invite you to join Facing History and Ourselves in the quest to learn the historical lessons for yourselves, and to urge, excite, and support our students in their attempts to make sense out of the chaos that has preceded us. We have the potential for greatness. Why not make certain that this potential is realized in our lifetime? Thank you.

A Brief Note about Committing to Fifth-Level Living[12]

March 2006

Where to direct one's energy is almost always a question of potential return or reward for having invested in the given activity. We consult values and norms, and consider the expectations of others; but finally, it is our notion about the payoff that leads us to a decision. Having a clear vision of what we want to achieve in a particular sphere of life serves to make this process easier. Our choices are made with a sense of true agency when we can see how our goals might be actualized. In truth, we do what we want to do. We have no trouble committing to a course of action when that action becomes the connection between wanting and having.

It is here that we make what I have termed "fifth-level commitments." This level of commitment is best described as "doing whatever it takes to make it happen." No longer will we vacillate and hover around lower levels of commitment; we quickly abandon such notions of "thinking about it," or "trying to do it," in favor of putting all our resources on the line to achieve the desired results.

You will never hear the person who is committed at the fifth level expressing concerns about how much one can do; he or she knows in advance to do what must be done. Nor will you find such a person hindered by boundaries, requirements, or social expectations. No, the truly committed person will find a way to make things happen in the service of meeting the desired goal. You have experience already that might not be immediately evident; but think about those times in your life when you have really wanted something for yourself or another person you've held in high esteem. In those instances you did not hesitate to make a fifth-level commitment.

Some years ago, I learned from my two daughters something about this commitment business. They came to me as a delegation, all of twelve and ten years of age at the time, but politically astute and aware of the need for negotiation. Their concern was this: "Dad, it is virtually impossible for kids to be able to get to school by eight o'clock in the morning. We need to make some adjustments."

After some discussion about the issues, I agreed to think about some alternatives. In the meantime, I said to them, we are planning a family trip to Disneyland next Saturday morning. In order to get there from where we lived in the Napa Valley, we had to leave at least by five o'clock in the morning. If I remember correctly, that conversation took place on Wednesday, so the Disneyland trip would take place in three days.

At three o'clock Saturday morning, I hear noises in the hallway outside our bedroom. I get up to investigate and find two children, completely dressed, having already eaten breakfast, cleaned the kitchen, and anxiously awaiting what in their minds is the late arrival of oversleeping parents! Talk about commitment!

Well, the lesson I learned then and there was that my daughters were symbolic of all of us. When we want to do it, it gets done. Angie and Becki, who were on record as having stated that they were convinced of the impossibility of being ready for school by eight o'clock, had demonstrated that early morning readiness was a matter of commitment.

The question we are forced to ask ourselves is simply this: What am I willing to commit to? The complexities of life argue strongly for more of us to make high-level commitments to improving the quality of our existence. I urge you to consider increasing your commitment to fifth-level living.

The Value of True Education[13]

Baccalaureate Sermon presented at Pacific Union College
Angwin, California

June 13, 1998

Earlier this week, I spoke to the graduating seniors of Polytechnic High School, a private school in Pasadena with a reputation for academic excellence. Nearly 100% of Poly graduates are accepted into the nation's best colleges and universities. This year, two Poly students were among 60 United States high school students selected by *USA Today* as Academic All-Americans. Such recognition bears witness to the claim that this school does, indeed, provide a superior education.

As part of the preparation for my talk, at their request, I met with a group of Poly seniors who were interested in knowing what I might say to them and their respective sets of parents, relatives, and friends. One of them said to me: "You have to know that all of us are smart." And, as we engaged in dialogue, it was apparent to me that this group of young people was quite able to process information with remarkable skill.

And yet, I wondered, are they aware of how this information might be applied in the context of life outside the realm of academia? Will they be able to wrestle successfully with the pertinent issues of their adult existence? With those thoughts in mind I asked about curriculum content that might prepare them to participate fully, as informed, concerned citizens, in a world faced with a plethora of social, political, moral, spiritual, ethical, legal, and interpersonal dilemmas.

They were not aware of any such content. None of their classes took them beyond high-level mastery of fundamental, as well as esoteric, subject matter. These young graduates can recall, recite, compute, analyze, synthesize, compose, articulate, interpret, decipher, and problem-solve better than most of us. The obvious question is: "Have they been truly educated? Do they merit the label of educated persons?" The answer, of course, depends upon the barometer used to measure their levels of education.

I've been told that there are those among us who have concluded that no person who lacks the ability to read and write the Chinese language can lay claim to this label. By that measure, Poly students, in the main, along with all the rest of us fall short of qualifying as educated persons. But there is another measuring rod we can employ.

To assess with any degree of accuracy how well educated you have become, it is essential to know how well acquainted you have become with the Savior of the world. Outside the context of a viable relationship with Christ, nothing of substance exists. How, you say, can he make such a bold statement? It is not so bold when you realize the facts of the matter.

Everything that we have, and the potential to have more, comes to us from the omniscient God of the universe. And so it is, those things which sustain, nurture, support, and guide us through life comes from Him who created each one of us to be His own. We choose whether or not we will be truly educated when we choose whether or not to follow Christ.

It is not enough to enroll in and attend classes at Pacific Union College. It is not sufficient to earn a place on the dean's list. Your acceptance into schools of medicine, dentistry, law, business or any one of hundreds of other professional or graduate study programs gives no cause to celebrate. No, these accomplishments, as fine as they are, do not prove that you have become educated persons. Nor is it a sign that you have earned the label when you are invited to join Phi Beta Kappa or the

Mensa society. Much like the Poly students, "you are smart," but you may or may not be educated.

Once you have made the decision to follow the lead of Christ, you begin to understand the value of true education. Your perception of yourself and your surround changes dramatically. You look out at the world through eyes that discern things differently than do those who follow their own dictates, or who misinterpret the teachings of Christ. You realize that even though you take up very little space in the universe, you can wield influence that will transform lives, and lead others to the threshold of their own understanding of the possibilities that true education brings. You sense that there is much more to this thing called life than adhering to the prevailing norms of society. You are motivated to challenge beliefs, policies, standards of behavior, and socially accepted practices that do not reflect the mind of Christ. You will have the stamina and willpower to address whatever version of the Sanhedrin awaits your appearance. In Acts 4:13, we read: "When they saw the courage of Peter and John and realized that they were unschooled, ordinary men, they were astonished and they took note that these men had been with Jesus." (From the New International Version)

As a truly educated person, you will know about, and appreciate, your own vast storehouse of ignorance. A most salient value of true education is that you have the opportunity to face and resolve what appears on the surface to be a real conundrum: The more I learn, the more I discern how little I really know!"

Not to worry. Choosing to be educated means also to accept the mantle of learner, a garment you will wear proudly and continuously throughout life. You will learn also about the particular gifts that are yours. And you will learn that comparing your gift to that of another is not required. We are all assigned by God to tasks He has planned for us to confront; it is His choice that I should do one thing and you another. Nobody is required to know it all.

Oddly enough I encountered a professor in my doctoral program who claimed to know it all. He said to our seminar group one afternoon that, if he ever stated that he did not know something, it was not that he didn't know, but that it was not known! My professor would have been well-advised to read along with us from Romans 12:3-6 "For by the grace given me I say to every one of you: Do not think of yourself more highly than you ought, but rather think of yourself with sober judgment, in accordance with the measure of faith God has given you. Just as each of us has one body with many members, and these members do not all have the same function, so in Christ we who are many form one body, and each member belongs to all the others. We have different gifts according to the grace given us. If a man's gift is prophesying, let him use it in proportion to his faith." (NIV)

A value without price is the peace of mind that comes from knowing God and His will in our lives. When you think about the emotional chaos that reigns within when we take over the responsibility for running our lives, when we assess the resultant toll on body and spirit, it is comforting to know that we can have peace by turning our lives over to One who has always known what we need, and how best it can be achieved.

You may have a favorite text related to peace; mine is Isaiah 26:3, and I like the King James version which puts it this way, "Thou wilt keep him in perfect peace whose mind is stayed on Thee." This was especially comforting to me when I faced the mobs in Little Rock and felt fear that I never knew existed. It was God's peace that reigned within me and made it possible for me to go forward with the fear stuck in my pocket.

The value of true education is seen clearly in the dialogue between two people who have chosen to speak the words given to them by God and not their own words. In my professional life, I meet a variety of people who struggle mightily with forces beyond their control. In those instances when I am willing to allow the word of God to hold sway, when the other person is open to hearing those words, the tenor of the conversation is different in kind and quality when compared to the exchanges that occur when God's presence is muted. Words are chosen with care; sharp edges are blunted.

A true education allows one to discern with clarity the gross difference between wisdom and folly. In Proverbs 15:21 we read: "Folly delights a man who lacks judgment, but a man of understanding keeps a straight course." (NIV) I like even better the Revised Standard version of that same text: "Folly is joy to him who has no sense, but a man of understanding walks aright." There are, and will be, myriad opportunities to determine what is folly and what is not as you continue your journey from the hilltop. Let it be said of you, as they said of Peter and John, "These people have been with Jesus."

True education allows you to live lives of substance, integrity, and forthrightness. And remember, acquiring a true education is not a passive activity; you need to work at it. More precisely, you need to work with God in the name of discovering and developing the potential that is inherently yours. Don't fret if you are unaware of what that potential might be; be assured, however, that God does have a plan for you.

In Acts 7:22, we read: "Moses was educated in all the wisdom of the Egyptians and was powerful in speech and action." We then read how Moses gets himself into big trouble and spends the next 40 years in the desert, learning about his potential. Some may have felt that he had already reached the mountaintop there in Egypt, but God knew better.

God knows better about you. He knows that more than anything else, you need a sure and certain knowledge of the Savior. Make this your quest, and you can wear the label of educated person, a truly educated person, with no fear of misrepresenting who you are.

"But whatever was to my profit I now consider loss for the sake of Christ. What is more, I consider everything a loss compared to the surpassing greatness of knowing Christ Jesus my Lord, for whose sake I have lost all things. I consider them rubbish, that I may gain Christ and be found in Him, not having a righteousness of my own that comes from the law, but that which is through faith in Christ—the righteousness that comes from God and is by faith. I want to know Christ and the power of his resurrection and the fellowship of sharing in his sufferings, becoming like him in his death, and so, somehow, to attain to the resurrection from the dead." Philippians 3: 7-11 (NIV)

Building Relationships: A Christian Perspective[14]

A talk presented at First United Methodist Church
Pasadena, California

Tuesday, January 27, 2004

The war correspondent, fatigued and weary in the wake of the chaos that defined the conflict around him, was moved to speak to the young boy as he came toward him. On the shoulders of this very determined young man was another child who appeared to be only slightly younger. "You are carrying quite a load, young man. Isn't he heavy?" "Naw, mister, he ain't heavy, he's my brother."

This response speaks to the power of relationship as filial bonds define it. It defines, as well, a quality of relationship that can be developed outside the narrow confines of biological ties. If we accept this vision of willingness to carry the weight of a sibling as our preferred objective, we can look closely at relationship as a way of interacting in this universe.

Relationship is not the same as social alliance, where people come together for some clearly specified, usually very personal or even selfish, reasons. Relationship is defined by unselfish commitment to the overall well being of another. Social alliance is tenuous, temporary, and tangential. Relationship is founded upon lasting principles that communicate, above all, continuing messages of love for the other person.

We, as a society of individuals, do not yet know how to be in relationship with each other. The social statistics are profound: marriages typically end in divorce, parents find it hard to co-exist with children, teachers are at war with students, employers are often at odds with workers. Newspapers are filled with stories about the tragic consequences that follow failed attempts at relationship.

But, we can learn how to be in relationship. We need to learn how to do this because our ability to maximize whatever potential is ours depends upon our having this skill. The only way we can effectively lift as we climb is to solve the puzzle of relationship. The surface interaction, the veneers of acceptance, the pseudo-relationship, all mitigate against forming healthy ties with others.

You see, in truth, we can only climb when we are pushed along, pulled along, supported by countless others. There is reciprocity here. To the degree that all the players understand this dynamic, learning and growing can take place; a lot of learning and growing when understanding is greatest, very little growth when understanding is limited. As we grasp the fundamentals of this arrangement, we increase our chances of moving closer to the essence of relationship. We get nearer to the point of knowing how to climb and lift, how to accept the help and support of others, and to provide the extended hand to those awaiting our assistance.

As Christian people, we have the distinct advantage of being able to review viable models to guide our choices in this arena. In general terms, mutual support has always been a staple of Christian existence. This legacy provides a rich repository of information—of guidelines, of direction, of ideas about substantive, meaningful connection with others.

My own experience as a young person growing up in Little Rock, Arkansas, included the benefit of having been pushed and pulled toward goals and objectives seen as essential for all young people. It was here that I was introduced to a saving God. It was within this context that I learned the value of working hard to succeed, and the concomitant value of helping others to do the same. I was impressed to no end by the golden rule: "Do unto others as you would have them do unto you."

You, no doubt, have your own stories to add to this list. The stories are potent and deserve to have a place in our conscious awareness. From the stories come the substance we use to keep leaning in the direction of relationship. There is danger in forgetting the messages the stories bring to us. As members of this western society we are privy to formulations that attempt to define who we are, and how we are supposed to be. Developmental theories speak to individuation, separation, independence, and to the gross pathology that exists in the absence of these hallowed virtues.

Don't rush to embrace this logic; it is culturally based, culturally biased. Interdependence is something to consider instead. Leaning on each other in the name of building a viable community of mutually concerned others has resonance for me. In the New Testament, Paul admonishes us in Philippians 2:4 to consider the needs of others. In many ways the whole of the bible includes messages that reflect Paul's thinking.

Your future success or failure is, in great measure, a function of how well you learn the lesson of relationship. We need each other! Psychologically we have an innate need to be in relationship. Our primary difficulty is our gross ignorance about the process, and a tendency to follow the drumbeat of selfishness and greed. Keep in mind that none of us take up very much room in the universe. We have little power and less authority. But together, united in vision and principle, we can fill up the interstitial spaces and exert an influence that moves us all beyond the ordinary.

I will end with a quote from *The Prophet* by Kahlil Gibran. He speaks to our need to recognize our interrelatedness.

"Like a procession you walk together towards your god-self. You are the way and the wayfarers. And when one of you falls down he falls for those behind him, a caution against the stumbling stone. Ay, and he falls for those ahead of him, who though faster and surer of foot, yet removed not the stumbling stone."

Can There Be Any Good Thing Here?[15]

September 2006

I was hesitant at first; the idea of yet another item on my agenda seemed impossible to even contemplate. But Beverly was insistent that I come by and see what was being done in the Tools For Tolerance For Educators Program. What I saw and heard when I finally decided to visit one of the programs convinced me to make room in my life for this experience. I witnessed the fervor and excitement of the team members who worked together with uncanny precision, the wonder and amazement on the faces of the participants, and the rich, substantive dialogue that spilled out of the classrooms into the hallways, even flowing up and down Pico Boulevard as we made intermittent forays to the local barbecue joint. In addition to that, there have been countless opportunities to interact and compare notes with presenters who bring varied backgrounds and myriad perspectives to the learning table. The most engaging feature for me has been the opportunity to draw my chair into the circle and expand my own fund of information, to increase my level of understanding about so many ideas, to see possibilities and potentials that were not yet on my radar screen, to know the world from the vantage point of different others.

It was not long after my initiation as a presenter that I was invited to share my story with Law Enforcement, the Hate Crimes Institute, the Library Program, Tools For Teens, and other groups as they were identified and invited to the Museum. One consistent thread woven throughout all of this has been the unquestioned value of each individual. As I have filled my designated space here, I have felt honored and embraced by those around me. This spirit of inclusion permeates the atmosphere and adds to the ambience in ways that encourages deeper reflection about the issues being dissected and analyzed. In such an environment, true learning can take place; it is hard to hide behind a carefully constructed mask when the invitation to join the fray is so genuinely proffered. And, for those who take full advantage of all that the programs present, the rewards are immediate and profound. Oh, there is pain involved in some of this, that goes almost without saying. No real learning comes without its measure of chaotic disruption, its insistence on challenging cherished points of view, its demand that addictions to habitual patterns of thought and behavior be exposed and excised. This combination of total positive regard and emphasis on real learning has proven to be one of the most significant weight-bearing pillars of the Museum programs.

It is here as well that one can find compelling, exciting discussions about difference in all of its manifestations. The simple truth: difference is, period! There is no need to explain, excuse, hide, ignore, or turn a blind eye to the variations on life's many themes. My appreciation for what transpires in this arena knows no bounds. In coming to the Museum I have found a place where the whole of me need not be altered to fit the tailored dimensions of some ideological construct that leaves little room for uniqueness. The celebration of difference adds a pleasing resonance to the multiplicity of sounds echoing from the walls.

Perhaps the other notion that must be underscored is that hope can be found in the interstitial spaces around this place. Hope that life can reveal the secrets that will inform us about the ways in which we can live together without fearing each other, hope that love can prove to the conqueror of evil it claims to be, hope that we can maximize the potential that lies dormant in the bone marrow, and that finally, hope will spring to life with vigor and crowd out the pernicious contenders that would have us kneel at the altar of hate and destruction. In no other place have I found the eclectic combination of elements that translate into such a viable expression of life at its fullest. My time here has been well spent thus far; I look forward to the next chapter.

In Search of An Open Mind[16]

Musings about a trip to Little Rock

Reflection Paper presented at Antioch University to my Society and the Individual class

March 2005

And so it was off to Little Rock to mingle with the Southern contingent and experience anew the rush of adrenaline that accompanies each of my forays into the delta. I work hard at erasing the images from *Five Smooth Stones* as I wander through the Dallas concourse, looking for the gate with the sign reading American Eagle to Little Rock, departing soon.

Funny how a mental map seems to be created with indelible ink when it comes to some things in life. My antennae are aroused when I see the cowboy scowl in my direction; was he upset because of the image beamed off my face into his cerebral computer? Will I have to engage in combat with this rough and ready soul because he would prefer that I not occupy space he has to enter? The moment passes without incident; without incident recorded for the public to see; not incidental for me, or Wild Bill either, I would suspect.

Soon enough I am whisked off to my hotel, where I am led to my quarters by a loquacious denizen of the region who floods my conscious awareness with tales of Benihana's excellence and my right to enjoy a 10% discount if I dine there tonight. With an exaggerated wave of both hands, he fends off my attempt to reward his bellhopping efforts, and tells me that "Mr. Ross said he would take care o'me."

I pray a silent prayer for the Rosses of the world and sit down at the desk to compose the speech I will deliver on the next day. How long should it be? There are seven pages of hotel stationery at the ready; the speech shall be 14 pages long (I shall use both sides, and I will write legibly). As I find my way to the body of this talk, to be presented to young scholars who will receive the Southwestern Bell Bates Scholarship, I sense a need to "get their attention." To that end I add dramatic flair, not at the sacrifice of solid content, but it occurs to me that these students of the '90s have feasted on fast-paced electronic inputs. They will require flash and dash, a bit of elan vital if you will.

And so it is settled. And at six a.m. on the morn of the day, I am required to visit a local television station to do a live feed for the Channel 11 news junkies who are abroad at that hour of the day. The anchors are folk who have mastered the art of "looking good on TV," and manage to ask some pertinent questions about my being in town. I have been prepped by the PR pro who guides Southwestern Bell through the turbulent waters of public scrutiny, and have my answers at the ready. I know the company line and it's a good one, I don't mind spouting it off. I get to name drop.

Since it's so early when we finish, I get to use one of their computers to record my scribblings from the night before. All goes well until the printout confirms that this is indeed a newsroom, and my script now resembles the rolled copy for a teleprompter: all in caps and less than single-spaced. How do they do that? Can't use it in any case, but I still have the hotel paper; that will have to suffice. And so it does.

I get a standing ovation and personal kudos from the CEO himself. It has been okay. Crazy at times. Like when Ross has to hear from one of the TV types: "You look just like Danny Glover" (he doesn't, really). And when Ross is not amused, he adds: "I mean it in the best way possible." But hey, this is America, where you never know what will flow your way.

On the Inauguration of Neal King as President of Antioch University[17]

Los Angeles, California

Speech given October 5, 2007

It has been said on more than one occasion, and given voice by more than a few observers among us, that where there is no vision, the people perish. Where there is little foresight, scant attention to meaningful detail, reckless abandon in the face of real human need, and a penchant for harboring the muses of greed and selfishness, there is, at the same time, the very distinct possibility that we may lose the right to inhabit this planet. If ever there was a reason to search diligently for those who would lead by honest example, who would demonstrate the value of a life of integrity, who would think critically, judge carefully, and live as a peer to all others in the universe, this is the hour. This is the time.

Some would argue that leaders are born; others might declare that leadership is a learned quality. I take no position in that debate. There are many who believe that good leaders are made of the "right stuff," and that the methods of identifying good leaders are to be found, not in science, but in the realms of art. After all, isn't it true that leadership style varies greatly? Some leaders are forceful and outspoken; others are quiet, almost demure. Some who lead are always out in front, leading, while others hang back, behind the troops. And we have to acknowledge that different situations demand unique leadership abilities.

How one finally arrives at the point of shouldering the responsibility of guiding others through the maze of life is of little consequence to me; but I am indeed interested in, and very concerned about, the motivating factors that propel some forward to offer themselves as shepherds. Yes, shepherds, because true leaders are those who understand the role to be one of watching out for the flock. Leaders who exemplify the position know intuitively that theirs is a sacred responsibility to be mindful of the needs of others. At the point position, the leader calls out rock, branch, stone, thorn, so that those who follow can avoid the obstacles that might impede progress along the trail. The leader prepares the way, and provides the encouragement and sustenance that the followers may require.

In the mind of the true leader is also found that which can only be described as the essence of the assignment, the core of leadership, if you will. And that is the unwavering commitment to the idea of the collective. It has never been a "we/they" dichotomy, but always an "us" for all who claim to be in charge.

And where is it that we will be led, those of us who depend upon the heads, the chiefs, the executives? In a world of reason and rational decision-making, the answer is clearly written on the walls of the universe: we lean in the direction of social justice for all.

At Antioch we are privileged to be ahead of the curve, so to speak. All who would be leaders here know in advance where the flock is headed. When I came to this university 14 years ago, I was excited to find so many likeminded individuals: people who cared about the essential issues of life; people who were willing to fight for those who could not fight for themselves; people who spoke for those whose voices had been muted—a group of concerned, involved citizens who could not rest until something was done to ease the pain felt by so many others around them.

We gather here today to inaugurate a leader of the Antioch community. We expect no less of him than we do of ourselves as we consider what must be done to right the ship of state—to solve the problems caused by uncertain and often debilitating pseudo-leadership at all levels of government; to educate a group of students willing to take the baton we hand off to them in this race to save ourselves from ourselves.

Fortunately, we have found a man who understands all of these things. And to the degree that his understanding may lag, we are fortunate to have a community of outspoken activists who will point him in the right direction. We do the leader a disservice when we allow him to founder, to wander into dangerous territory, or to forget the principles that brought him to our attention in the first place.

In my estimate, there is little risk of such happenstance with Neal King. He has demonstrated already that his vision for us is based on lucid thought about the challenges of the future. His choice to accept this mantle is not a casual decision, but one borne of considered thought about the ways in which he can continue to follow the spirit of Antioch, and in so doing, lead us along pathways yet to be discovered as we move deeper into this 21st Century.

I speak these words not so much as proven statements of truth, but more as clarion calls to all assembled here to accept personal responsibility for making them come true if they are not yet realized. We need Neal King, and he needs us. Together we can make Antioch University, Los Angeles the beacon of light that can and will illuminate even the darkest corner of our surround. As we go forth today from this place, let us keep in mind the admonition: Where there *is* vision, the people flourish.

Letter to Sen. Barack Obama, Democratic Presidential Candidate[18]

March 25, 2008

Dear Senator Obama,

We are two of your most ardent supporters here in Pasadena, California, and want you to know how much we appreciate what you are attempting to do for this country. Your run for the presidency has helped all of us to see more clearly the potential for greatness that the United States possesses. As you continue to rise above the level of party politics and refuse to engage in the primal behavior displayed by your current Democratic opponent, we are energized to take a more active role as citizens of this republic. There have been times when it seemed feasible to vacate these shores for some more hospitable place to live and work, but with your willingness to confront the defenders of the status quo and to offer a real opportunity for change, we are motivated to help in any way we can.

Fifty years ago I (Terrence) joined the group known to the world as The Little Rock Nine. It was our intent then to try to help this country build a more equitable society. The response to our efforts was not encouraging, and as the years have passed, it seems that too few citizens want to challenge the notion of business as usual. It is your candidacy, however, that has given my wife, Rita, and I renewed hope that real change is possible.

Thank you for taking on such an important task, for helping

us to see beyond the ordinary, and to rekindle the fires of hope for a better society. We applaud the public stand you took in the wake of the furor surrounding words spoken by Pastor Wright, and we appreciate the fact that you were willing, in the words of one commentator, to speak to us as if we were adults.

We know the toll that a venture such as this one can take on a family, and we want you to know that we include you and Michelle and your daughters in our prayers. It is our fervent hope that you will be able to lead this country as its next president; we will do all we can to make certain that our hopes are realized. As we shared with our Pasadena friends that we would be writing this letter to you, they said to be sure to tell him that they too are working hard to convince any and all to cast their votes for you.

Sincerely,
Terrence and Rita Roberts

President Barack Obama: Thoughts and Reflections[19]

A Pre-Inauguration Essay

It was January 2008, and I was somewhere on the East Coast when I had a sudden thought that I had better book rooms and schedule a flight to Washington, D.C., for the inauguration of President Obama. Immediately I phoned my wife in Pasadena to tell her about my inspiration. She was happy to hear from me, but not very optimistic that this was the most rational choice I could have made. I was, however, beyond rationality at that point. Something inside me was insistent that this was the most prudent choice I could make. And so it happened. My own optimism grew steadily as I watched the drama of the primary contest and then later, the race for the White House.

The election of Barack Obama seemed to be a sure thing. If I were asked to explain how I came to see things this way, I would be unable to tell you, because for me it was not a cerebral function; this was purely visceral. In retrospect, I can cite events that stand out in time and space, events that could have derailed the Obama candidacy. In each case he was able to ride out the storms, and as he did so, my convictions about his destiny to become the president grew stronger.

As I read *Dreams from My Father* and *The Audacity of Hope*, I found evidence of a man committed to service, one aware of his own abilities, but not focused on his own ego needs. His mantra of change was borne of his concern for all of us who live in America. His consistent choice to treat all others as peers demonstrated clearly his intent to model how to live comfortably with difference of any kind. Here was a leader filled with conviction that we could be better than we had been, much better even than we had ever before imagined.

I would not describe Barack Obama as a politician, although it is apparent that he understands the political process. In my estimate he is a statesman. And by this I mean that he is willing to accept the sacred responsibility of guarding the public trust. His is not a quest for personal gain or acclaim; he simply wishes to serve the people. How long have we needed such a person!

My emotional response to his election was nothing short of prolonged and sustained elation. On that Tuesday night in November, I was able to look back 51 years and see the Nine of us contending with the hard, unrelenting edges of racism in Little Rock. The contrasting images of those two scenes—a man of African heritage slated for the White House and mobs of angry white people yelling virulent racist invective toward nine young people of African heritage—was stark indeed. At the same time, I was able to conclude with a sense of delicious irony that our struggle had not been in vain. I admit to feeling a bit of pride even that we had helped to usher in this chapter of American history. It is important to remind those who would see historical events as disparate elements in a chaotic universe that all things that ever happen are simply, and merely, antecedent to all other things that may happen.

Another thought surfaced as I stayed up late to bask in the afterglow: What if some of my more liberal friends decide that the war against racism has been won? Will they decide to turn their energies elsewhere? Will they look for more urgent causes to champion? My optimistic side tells me that they will stay firmly grounded and continue to battle this egregious reality. But my realistic side says, don't be so certain.

What is true beyond doubt is that racist ideology has been dealt a serious blow. Our task now is to stamp out the remnants, find the encampments, and nullify the effects of the continuing rhetoric. This is especially needful given the e-traffic on websites and blogs of dubious character and, in some cases, of pure evil intent. I have this nagging feeling that, unless we remain vigilant, unless we maintain the keen awareness that the battle against the ideology of racism requires continued effort, we will allow this pernicious evil to spawn even more adherents. Perhaps more importantly, the need to root out the systemic elements that have been allowed to accumulate over the centuries will falter for lack of attention. We cannot give in to complacency. Our future demands that we act with quickened resolve.

A most significant part of the change that President Obama has promised is embodied within himself. The face he presents to the world speaks volumes about who we are as a people. Enough of us were able to sense this moment in time as one that could not be passed by, and we acted with alacrity by casting our ballots and urging others to do the same. On the day after the election, I read a newspaper story about students at Crenshaw High School in Los Angeles. Some of the students interviewed spoke at length about the need to take education seriously, to pay attention to life's potentials. Already the "Obama Effect" was in play.

I envision young people across lines of race, culture, ethnicity, and economic circumstances looking at our new president and deciding to alter their choice making processes. I can sense older people in our society recalibrating their racial barometers, extending their mental, psychological, social, and physical reach to take advantage of heretofore "hidden" opportunities.

Our place on the world stage has been spotlighted anew as well. The reported responses from world leaders, from citizens of other countries, from hamlets and villages all over this globe have been uniformly and consistently upbeat in their assessment of the future with President Obama at the helm in America.

No longer do I fear in-depth political dialogue with foreign nationals on my trips abroad. It is no longer necessary to prepare mentally for the smirks and caustic comments about our collective political insanity; and I can even expect to be congratulated for finally getting it right! Personally I am joyous about the possibilities that await us, as once again we take a favored position among the nations of the world.

Last year, 2007, in Chicago, I met Michelle Obama when I delivered the keynote address for the annual fund-raising dinner sponsored by the Chicago office of Facing History and Ourselves. Ms. Obama was on the board of directors, and introduced me on the program. I was excited to have the opportunity to share a table with her and some of her friends, and saw instantly that she was a woman who knew how to connect with others. She is affable, highly intelligent, personable, and most of all, fun to be around! As I consider the tenor of the White House-to-be, I am overjoyed to know that the Obama family will be in residence.

Earlier this year, I was reacquainted with Michelle Obama, and I met our future president as well, when the two of them came to Pasadena for a fund-raising event. I was impressed with Senator Obama's grasp of the issues facing this country. He seemed to be cognizant of needs at all levels of our society, and he was open to input from those of us assembled at the gathering. This was just further proof to me that my Washington, D.C., reservations would be put to good use.

And now, a word about the First Family: Recently a friend asked me, what did you think about first when the election was decided? No hesitation for me on that one: I said Malia and Sasha! Why? Because my grandsons, PJ and Austin will grow up with near age-group peers in residence at the White House. Their world view will be 180 degrees removed from the worldview I started with in 1941. As the Obama children roam the halls of the White House, as their every move is chronicled for all to see, PJ and Austin will be among the group of onlookers; they will see with their own eyes and hear with their own ears images and sounds that declare a new world of possibility.

And, remarkably enough, it will not be new to them at all! That's the beauty of the whole thing. My grandsons will not be burdened with all the baggage that was mine to carry. They will have much more opportunity to maximize the potential for growth and development that was in place at their birth. They will have a set of experiences void of the raw racism faced by my generation.

I have often said of the office of President of the United States that whoever occupies that space sets a tone for the country. He (or she at some point) dictates in large measure how all of us respond to issues both large and small. And while the president is the one most charged with that responsibility, the First Family is very much involved in the process. The Obama family has already begun to set a tone that has positive reverberations throughout the country. Their example as loving parents who care deeply for each other, their concern for the welfare and well-being of Malia and Sasha, their close ties to extended family members, and their choice to live by faith is instructive and inspirational to all of us. When we can release anxiety and fear, and learn to develop our higher order thoughts and emotions, we become a better people. I feel strongly that the Obama family will lead us in that direction.

But, know without doubt that none of this can happen unless we join forces with the President and his family. This means in practical terms that we must take personal inventory of our skills and abilities, and determine how best to use them in the service of building a new America.

Exclusion is out. Inclusion is the preferred mode. One salient task in this regard is the erasure of all lines of demarcation from our own mental maps. As we learn to live as peers in this universe, we can pool our energies to build, create, develop, explore, resolve conflicts, and find new ways to use the former political and social weapons of mass destruction. In fact, when you think about it, we have, collectively, enough explosive firepower to blow up the globe. We can take out Earth! As we follow Obama's lead, we can discover how to think differently about these issues. We might even find that learning how to live in peace is possible!

Perhaps that is too much of a stretch, but I think my point is well made. If we determine that we want to be involved in activities that uplift, support, and encourage people to be the best they can be, we will do so. Bottom line: It's up to us. We have made a spectacular choice in placing Barack Obama in a prime leadership position. Now we have to be followers who believe in the leader and his potential.

America, our wake-up alarm has sounded; a new day has dawned. What kind of day it will be cannot be trusted to chance. There are those among us who say time will take care of all problems, all issues. But time is neutral; time alone does nothing. It is only *action* in time and space that makes a difference.

The alarm call is for action of the highest caliber. We can rebuild our failing infrastructure. We can create systems of education for all children. We can develop a healthcare system that leaves no one uncovered. But we can only do these things if we all cooperate.

When President Obama sounds his own clarion call for citizen involvement, get involved. When the demand is there for expertise, offer it. If you don't feel prepared for any of this, tool up. And, if by dint of circumstance and lack of opportunity you find yourself unable to contribute anything of substance, know in advance that your moral support for those who are more able is substantive to the extreme.

In the midst of the presidential campaign, when myriad forces were arrayed against the Obamas, I prayed for their success. When the voices of opposition were loudest, I often felt like shouting out to them, "You don't deserve a man of such merit!" But I am encouraged today. I am hopeful that we will, as a nation, rise above the pettiness that too often defines our character. We have made this necessary first step, but it is just that: a first step. Let's prove to ourselves and to all others around the globe that we can, indeed, complete the journey.

Endnotes

1. Some of you know already that the skin of polar bears is black, which allows for a greater absorption of heat. Life in the frigid arctic would be tenuous at best if not for this fact. The polar bear coat is made up of clear, colorless hairs that appear white, or yellow, depending upon the light angle and/or the viewers' position. Feel free to verify my statements; but stop short of trying to prove this by close examination of any given polar bear! Hair or color notwithstanding, polar bears are not likely to take kindly to such scrutiny.

2. As I stated in this book's preface, I have included these two entries about Little Rock because they contain nuanced differences that together make a complete narrative.

   For those who wish to read more in depth about my Little Rock experience, I recommend my book *Lessons from Little Rock*, published in October 2009 by the Butler Center for Arkansas Studies.

3. During my tenure as Assistant Dean of the UCLA School of Social Welfare, I was invited by the Pasadena-Altadena chapter of the NAACP to give a keynote address at their annual dinner. I decided to talk about life in the 21st Century with a specific focus on how to cope with our legacy of racism. You will quickly see in reading this entry how certain thought processes have been a part of my world over these last 20-odd years. As an American citizen it would be strange not to have such thoughts given the legal, social, cultural, and psychological reality that has been ours to share. My aim was not to cast blame or to find fault but to offer ways of coping with this ubiquitous reality.

4. In 1991, by a Senate vote of 52-48, Clarence Thomas became the second African American appointed to the U.S. Supreme Court. The appointment followed highly publicized, politically charged Senate hearings in which black attorney Anita Hill, a former federal employee working for Thomas, testified that he had sexually harassed her. Thomas adamantly denied the allegations.

   As a justice, Thomas has aligned himself with the high court's conservative justices. African-American political groups have criticized him for his votes in cases such as those dealing with school desegregation, race-based redistricting of voting districts, and racial quotas.

   A decade after his appointment, I found myself angered by his court votes and public persona. It led me to write this criticism.

   I must say, even today the man remains a virtual enigma. There is a line in the film "A Soldier's Story" spoken by a character who seems to be exasperated by the actions of one of his compatriots. He questions: "What kind of Negro are you anyway?" Perhaps that is the question I want to ask Justice Thomas. And maybe there are more questions outside my ken of awareness at the moment. In any case, this is an area of interest for me especially so because the stakes are so high. Think about it, Clarence is one of only nine people who by law and custom wield an extraordinary amount of power in our society.

   I admit to having ideological differences with Justice Thomas, I admit to having virtually nothing in common with the man, and I admit to being frustrated with my inability to order him off the Court! And why single out just one of the nine? Well, it mainly regards my notions about who should have replaced Thurgood Marshall. Absent that fact I would be, perhaps, a bit less enraged; but I think still I would harbor massive resentment.

5. There I was, seated on an airplane headed toward the East Coast having just departed from LAX prior to the era of iPods and before I could afford BOSE earphones. I did, however, have an unused legal pad and before too long I was totally immersed in this project. I have been fascinated by Clarence for a long time and it seemed timely for me to put on paper the thoughts racing around inside my head. You see, the seat now occupied by Justice Thomas belonged to Thurgood Marshall. When I finally accepted the reality that Clarence had indeed been selected to fill

Justice Marshall's seat, my anger and frustration began to build. How could George the First have been so blind? And yet, there it was, the seat reserved for a man who had fought so hard and for so long for real justice in this country was now to be the resting place for this interloper!

I showed the handwritten manuscript to my daughter, Angela, and after she read through it, she said, "Dad, you were angry when you wrote this." Not an accusation, no indictment, just a simple statement of fact. She read me well; I was angry, angry because I felt the memory of Justice Marshall was being tarnished, angry because Clarence seemed to be incapable of even understanding what was required of a Supreme Court Justice in these United States of America, angry because I had no power to reverse this insidious wrong, and angry because the future promised more such appointments to the highest court in the land.

My anger has subsided somewhat, but I feel trapped by a system that seems to cater to those who ignore the realities of life in favor of fictional facsimiles. I am reminded of the card-playing crows in *The Wiz* whose mantra was, "You can't win, you can't break even, and you can't get out of the game!" Given this very sobering reality, I have resolved to learn how best to navigate this terrain. Stay tuned for more on this subject!

And I hope you have stayed tuned because Clarence has managed to use his position on the court to render myriad mind-boggling decisions. For example, on June 22, 2009, as I was preparing this manuscript for submission to the publisher, Clarence came charging to the fore with yet another mind-boggling dissent in the Court's 8-1 ruling in support of continuing the Voting Rights Act. According to Clarence's logic, the entire voting rights provision should be thrown out as unconstitutional. And then, on June 25, 2009, again as the lone dissenter, Clarence ruled against the thirteen-year-old girl who was strip searched by her school administrators in their quest to find what turned out to be non-existent drugs. The school authorities has acted on a tip from another student and seemed hell bent on finding the contraband even to the point of having the young girl shake out her panties; perhaps motivated by the fact that this particular student had given them credible tips before? At any rate, in a true WTF moment, Clarence cited this as a ruling that would give all the thirteen-year-old druggies in the country a new way to beat the system.

Can you even imagine Thurgood Marshall taking such a ridiculous position? And here we are, eight years after I began this essay, still raging about Clarence and his madness. When will it end? Is there any reason to believe it ever will? I must say I certainly hope so. As a country we deserve better. Since we now have a president who thinks deeply about such matters, maybe the court will be refashioned, reshaped to include justices who give a rip about justice.

6. When I first learned about the death of Daisy Bates, I sat down and penned these lines. It was my thought that I might be called upon to speak words about her and about her relationship to the Little Rock Nine. It was also a time for me to recollect, to consider the impact of this dedicated civil rights activist upon my life and the lives of countless others. As fate would have it, during the time she was eulogized in Arkansas, I was in Washington, D.C., to receive the Congressional Gold Medal. One of our group of nine, Ernie Green, was commissioned to appear on our behalf, and I gave him a copy of these remarks.

   We forget, often that death is very much a part of the life cycle. It becomes a necessary marker in time and space for all of us at some point. It is well to remember Daisy as one who lived a full life worthy of celebration.

7. During one of the many public gatherings in honor of the passage of forty years since the uprising at Central High School in Little Rock, Arkansas, I was invited to address an audience at Philander Smith College. And so, on September 27, 1997, I found myself standing before an assembled group of hundreds on the south lawn of the College. It was a place I was more than familiar with and felt twinges of nostalgia along with a peace of mind that comes with being "at home." Many of my schoolmates from years past were present as were former teachers and mentors. Family members were scattered throughout the crowd, and the other eight members of the Little Rock Nine shared the dais with me. On the stage that morning as well was President and Mrs. Clinton. In fact, one of my assignments was to introduce President Clinton as the speaker to follow me on the program.

At the conclusion of my talk I did invite President Clinton to come forth and he began by saying that perhaps he should have hired me as one of his speech writers. In one of those cruel twists of fate, my remarks to the audience had been well received, but the subsequent statements of the President fell flat. He relied upon other speech writers who had failed to read the audience with any degree of clarity. Remarks that may have been better suited to a less well-educated or less socially conscious group did not find receptive listeners. I can imagine that those preparing the President's speech had mental images of black people as a monolithic group suffering from gross social pathologies. Nothing could have been farther from the truth on that day at Philander Smith College.

8. In the same week I delivered the talk at Philander Smith College, I wrote the following op-ed piece for the Arkansas Democrat-Gazette, the daily paper in Little Rock. It was reprinted first in *Lessons from Little Rock,* my memoir published in October 2009 by the Butler Center for Arkansas Studies. I include it here as a way of seeking wider readership, and to underscore the point I feel is still most salient: we have not yet reached Nirvana.

   Race relations in America, the specter of racism most recently seen on a national scale in the presidential race of 2008, continuing "incidents" around issues of race, all speak to the need to resolve the basic problems. Our task is clear, at least to me. We need to face the fact that many of our citizens and institutions still operate using race as a focal point for decision making.

9. In 2005 the United States Postal Service issued a series of stamps commemorating the civil rights struggle in America. One of those stamps honored the Little Rock Nine.

10. In March 2007, I was invited to attend a program honoring Philander Smith College athletes but was unable to make the trip to Little Rock at that time. It seemed to be such an important event that I decided to send a letter to be read to the group. My relationship with the College has its origins in the early 1940s when I played on the campus as a young boy. During the chaos in 1957 it was Philander Smith College faculty and students who

helped our small group of nine manage the first weeks of school when we were denied entrance to Central High.

Today I feel strongly about supporting the educational agenda of the college as a tribute to all that was done on my behalf those many years ago. In my remarks to the athletes, I attempt to convey a sense of that history as I urge them to take full advantage of the opportunities available to them.

11. A few years ago I learned about Facing History and Ourselves and was excited to discover this organization dedicated to illuminating history for teachers and students. Today I sit on the board of trustees as testament to my growing commitment to the ideals of this program. Annual fund raising dinners are sponsored by all of the regional offices of Facing History and the talk that follows is one I delivered in 2002 for the Los Angeles office. I have since had the pleasure of speaking at dinners held in Chicago, Cleveland, Memphis, and San Francisco.

    Please indulge me as I invite you to explore this organization for yourself. Find out just what Facing History is all about. I guarantee you that you will not be disappointed as you learn about the national and international scope of programming offered by this very creative and forward-thinking organization. The web site is: facinghistory.org. Or, you may contact Facing History by writing to the national office at: 16 Hurd Road, Brookline, MA 02445.

12. Throughout this text you have read some of my thoughts about commitment. I have encouraged students, admonished administrators, and urged individuals to consider making "fifth level" commitments to whatever might be the chosen courses of action. Much of my discourse about this has come in the context of explaining the "four-step process" but also I have underscored the simple necessity of being committed to something!

    In this brief note to follow, I have focused my attention yet again on the need for us to consider carefully the need for high level commitment. Why so much coverage for this topic? A good question, to be sure. My answer is that in the short span of life, a lot of our vital energy is squandered because there is no plan for its use. I am biased toward the fruitful use of all resources at our disposal and one of the ways to make this happen is to make a conscious commitment to do so. As you will see in this short piece, I am convinced that adult human beings do exactly what they want to do, and since this is the case, why not choose to do that which adds to the health and well-being of all of us?

13. In the summer of 1998 I was invited to deliver the baccalaureate sermon to the graduating seniors of Pacific Union College in Angwin, California. A private, Seventh-day Adventist liberal arts school, the college is located in the hills above St. Helena at the northern end of the Napa valley. I had lived in the area and was affiliated with the College during a ten-year stretch from 1975 to 1985 while I was Director of Mental Health Services at the St. Helena Hospital and Health Center in Deer Park, California, just down the hill from Angwin.

    Any opportunity to address an audience of young minds usually gets my full attention, and I was more than delighted to accept the invitation. And, as always, the big question was, what to say to this group on the verge of entering the world as newly minted college graduates? Eventually I settled on the theme of "true education." For a long time I have thought that most of what we consider to be education is not truly education but perhaps would be better described as an "unreasonable facsimile." Unreasonable because too many so-called educated persons seem not to know much at all!

    I must admit here that I am taking a big risk with an indictment of this magnitude but I trust that my writings about this theme will help to prove my point. If you are a Christian believer, you will, perhaps have less difficulty with the positions I promote in this sermon. In any case, I leave it to you, the reader, to come to your own conclusions. Allow me to say also, that I remain open to learning and growing in my own quest to understand better what it means to be a spiritual being. For as much as we are physical, mental, psychological, social, political, sexual, and communal beings, we are also spiritual.

14. For a brief period in our lives, my wife and I were members of the First United Methodist Church in Pasadena, California. In 2004 I was invited to address a group of members at a forum sponsored by the church. I chose to talk about building relationships in the context of Christian life. As you well know from reading previous entries in this text, I am convinced of the need for us to build

viable relationships. In fact, I am on record here as having said that healthy, growing dyads can be the essential building blocks of any society. This rings especially true in my head when we consider a community of Christian people.

A dynamic, involved group of people who know how to relate to each other in healthy ways speaks volumes about their belief system. Not only do they support each other in terms of meeting life's exigencies, but in so doing they model possibilities for others. This, in part, constitutes a pattern of Christian living. I, for one, find this to be an exciting thought.

15. Beverly LeMay is an educator in the Tools for Tolerance program sponsored by the Museum of Tolerance in Los Angeles. For a period of some months, perhaps even as much as a year or more, she had implored me to participate in the Tools program. I was too busy, no time, little interest, I told her, until one day she said: "Look, if you come and take a look, I will buy you lunch." Perhaps she caught me on a day when my nutritional needs were unmet, or perhaps my curiosity level was a bit higher, but in any case, I took her up on the offer.

    At this point, several years later, I am still involved in the programs at the Museum. If you are in the area, drop by and see for yourself what goes on here. I think you will be surprised and delighted.

16. At Antioch University, Los Angeles, where I taught for fifteen years, students in the mandatory Society and the Individual class were required to write a short reflection paper each week. During one quarter I had to miss one class meeting to travel to Little Rock to deliver a talk. The following entry is my reflection paper; I promised the class that since I had to be absent, I would bring back a reflection paper to inform them about my experience.

    In thinking about including this paper as part of the manuscript, I pondered the notion of inviting you, the readers, to write your own reflection papers each week. It is a valuable learning tool to help you focus on your own thought patterns and it can, over time, serve as a barometer of your growth and development. It is not absolutely necessary to share what you write with others, although if you have a cadre of trusted friends, they could be a group who could offer intriguing feedback. In any case, think about it.

17. I retired from Antioch University, Los Angeles on June 30, 2008, and now consider myself in some sort of transition period. The following piece written for the inauguration of Antioch's new president, Neal King, serves as a transition from this volume to whatever may follow. I have ideas floating around non-stop and it will be interesting to see what develops.

    I was chosen to speak on behalf of the faculty at Antioch and counted it an honor to have been thus selected. In working out the specifics for this talk, I had to consider what my colleagues might want to have voiced aloud. Also, I was charged with the responsibility of setting a tone for ongoing presidential-faculty interactions. At least that was my understanding.

    And so, here we are at the final offering, and I find myself wanting to say more and to say it better. But, there will be other opportunities for us to communicate. For now, put yourself in the audience at the Presidential inauguration and listen to the spoken words.

18. In March 2008, my wife and I sent a letter to the Obamas voicing our support of their quest to assume the highest office in the land. I have included that letter here as part of the introduction to my essay which follows the letter.

19. Before this manuscript was ready for submission to a publisher, Barack Obama was elected to become the 44th President of the United States of America. From my vantage point, that was an event that demanded a written response from me. What follows is an essay seen and read for the first time by readers of this book.

    For a long time I have felt that now President-elect Obama brings to us, the collected citizens of this republic, an opportunity to realize more completely the potential that is ours. The potential to take the elements we have—genetic endowments, visionary ideals, natural resources, true patriotism, seemingly indefatigable spirits, and a sense of destiny—and combine them all into a reality unfettered by specious lines of demarcation, and not vitiated by the greed and selfishness that has so recently served to undermine the economic future of our nation.

If you have found this book helpful, point your browser to www.parkhurstbrothers.com